Keyboarding for Computer Success

Jerry W. Robinson, Ed.D.
Former Keyboarding Instructor
Moeller High School
Cincinnati (OH)

Jack P. Hoggatt, Ed.D.
Professor, Department of
Business Communication
University of Wisconsin
Eau Claire (WI)

Jon A. Shank, Ed.D.
Professor of Education
Robert Morris College
Coraopolis (PA)

Lee R. Beaumont, Ed.D.
Professor of Business, Emeritus
Indiana University of Pennsylvania
Indiana (PA)

T. James Crawford, Ph.D., Ll.D.
Professor of Business/Education, Emeritus
Indiana University
Bloomington (IN)

Lawrence W. Erickson, Ed.D.
Professor of Education, Emeritus
University of California
Los Angeles (CA)

Business Education lost a dedicated friend and teacher in 1997 with the passing of Dr. Jerry W. Robinson. Dr. Robinson had completed his manuscript for this book before his untimely death.

JOIN US ON THE INTERNET
WWW: http://www.thomson.com
EMAIL: findit@kiosk.thomson.com   A service of I(T)P®

South-Western Educational Publishing
an International Thomson Publishing company I(T)P®

Cincinnati • Albany, NY • Belmont, CA • Bonn • Boston • Detroit • Johannesburg • London • Madrid
Melbourne • Mexico City • New York • Paris • Singapore • Tokyo • Toronto • Washington

Managing Editor:	Karen Schmohe
Production Coordinator:	Jane Congdon
Development:	Penworthy Learning Systems
Production:	CompuText Productions, Inc.
Design:	Grannan Graphic Design, Ltd.
Art/Design Coordinator:	Michelle Kunkler
Marketing Manager:	Tim Gleim
Marketing Coordinator:	Lisa Barto
Manufacturing Coordinator:	Carol Chase

PHOTO CREDITS:

viii: Printer: Photo courtesy of Hewlett-Packard Company

ix: Printer: Courtesy of Apple Computers, Inc.

1, 2, 5, 11-14, 16, 18, 21, 22, 24, 27, 30, 32, 34, 37, 38, 40, 44, 50, 52, 54, 56, 58, A-11: Greg Grosse

4, 7: 1977 PhotoDisc, Inc.

I(T)P ®

South-Western Educational Publishing is a division of International Thomson Publishing Inc. The ITP logo is a registered trademark used herein under license by South-Western Educational Publishing.

ISBN: 0-538-68584-0

01 02 03 04 05 06 07 08 09 00 D 05 04 03 02 01 00 99 98

Printed in the United States of America

Microsoft® and Windows® are registered trademarks of Microsoft Corporation.

COREL® and WordPerfect® are registered trademarks of Corel Corporation or Corel Corporation Limited in Canada, the United States, and/or other countries.

Preface

Keyboarding has become a universal writing skill. A high percentage of people in all walks of life use a computer keyboard to simplify and speed up their work. No matter what career you choose or what jobs you get along the way, a computer keyboard is likely to be the center of your communication.

Reporters, short story writers, poets, and novelists compose at computer keyboards. Many musicians use the computer keyboard to compose and arrange music, and artists use the keyboard for graphic design.

Keyboarding: A Universal Skill

Students, for example, from elementary school through college use their keyboarding skill to prepare school assignments. Many former students say that, next to English, keyboarding is the most useful skill they learned in school.

Communication is often called "the central nervous system" of business and industry. Though communication starts in the brain, it most often moves through the fingers to a keyboard that converts ideas into memos, letters, reports, and the like. These messages may be sent as hard copy through the mail, or they may be sent electronically as e-mail or faxes. Operating a computer keyboard and mouse, people everywhere take advantage of the Internet's infinite connections (see pp. iv-v) for education, entertainment, information, and profit. Someday we'll likely find ways to organize the Net's vast, dynamic stores of data, giving even more of us good reasons to navigate the Web at home, at school, and at work.

Getting the Most out of Computers

To get maximum value from a computer's high-speed output, the user must be competent at the input end—the keyboard. A person who can type 50 words a minute produces in half the time the same amount of work as someone who can key only 25 words a minute. Furthermore, the person who can type only 25 words a minute often has to think about which key to tap. The person who can key 50 words a minute is free to think about "bigger things," such as the content of the message keyed. Some people say that accuracy of input makes no difference because errors can be corrected quickly and easily on a computer. The fact remains, though, that the quickest, easiest error to correct is the one that is not made.

The Book Is New; Method Is Tried and True

This book balances up-to-the-minute content with a presentation style that has been tried and found true for 75 years. The 30 lessons are designed to develop basic keying (input) skills, including keying from script, rough-draft, and statistical copy and using standard proofreader's marks. Thus, users of the book are prepared to (1) apply their skills to the preparation of documents and (2) improve their skills even more as they use them.

Basic keying skill consists of fluent manipulation of letter, figure/symbol, and service keys by "touch" (not watching fingers). The following features of keyboard learning and practice are the basis for this book:

- Presents two alphabet or figure keys in each new-key lesson to ensure mastery of keyboard operation. (Four symbol keys—to be learned at the acquaintance, rather than the mastery, level—are presented in each symbol-key lesson, except Lesson 28. It contains symbols associated with computer language but rarely used in running copy.)

- Delays keying skill on the top row until correct technique and an essential level of keying skill have been developed.

- Uses scientific, computer-controlled drills to develop maximum skill in minimum time.

- Employs paragraphs that are *triple-controlled* for copy difficulty. Copy is rated as easy, low average, or average on the basis of (1) syllables per word, (2) keystrokes per word, and (3) percentage of common versus uncommon words.

- Stresses keying technique first (without timing); then speed of manipulation; and accuracy of keyed copy last. This technique-first/accuracy-last plan is in harmony with skill-learning principles and research findings.

Don't Miss These Bonus Features!

Large amounts of related learning round out this keyboarding book (see pp. vi and vii): (1) an introduction to the Internet; (2) useful information about *Windows 95*; (3) basic operations of word processing software, citing *Microsoft Word* and *Corel WordPerfect* as examples; (4) a short tutorial for operating the numeric keypad; (5) information for understanding and preventing repetitive stress injury; (6) basic memo, letter, and report formats and word processing features; and (7) a handy guide to English mechanics.

The Internet is changing the way people communicate and learn. The number of people using the Internet grows every day. If you are not yet among the millions of drivers on the Information SuperHighway, or Internet, this article puts you behind the wheel. Mastering a computer keyboard will put you in high gear.

The power of the Internet ties closely with using a computer keyboard. To create and post e-mail messages and "attachments," you use a keyboard. To search the vast Internet for something specific, you key words and phrases to define the search. If someone says "visit www dot . . . on the 'Net,'" you must type **www.** and all the other address characters.

The more skilled you are, the less you have to think about what keys to tap. Instead, you can keep your mind on the Internet and the stuff it contains. Learn to operate the keyboard mostly by touch (without looking at your fingers). Continue improving your keying technique—the secret behind fast, accurate typing.

What Is the Internet?

Connections. If you use the Internet, you have connections. The Internet is a network of computer networks. It is millions of computers all over the world, each linked electronically to each other. The links make certain types of information stored on any one of those computers available to all the others.

To describe how much information is at hand on the Internet, we use words like *huge* and *immense* and *stupendous* and *vast*. What kinds of information? you may wonder. All kinds. You (or anyone else) probably can't name a subject that's *not* on the Internet. With millions of users around the globe and tons of information ready for them, the Internet serves untold purposes. This list gives a few examples of things you might do on the Internet:

- take a course online
- buy a T-shirt
- promote your small business
- look for a job
- get up-to-the-minute news

How Does It Work?

Is using the Internet like looking up topics in a humongous library? Not exactly. You see, the information is unorganized and dynamic (always changing). Using the Internet is fun because you never know what you will find. At the same time, you must keep track of the places you go to on the Internet if you ever hope to go there again!

The Internet was made for information to go from point A (a sending computer) to point B (a receiving computer), along a path. It works like the post office: Information is put into an Internet "envelope," and the sender's computer puts an address on it. Another computer reads the address and passes the information to the next computer, and so on. Information going to many different addresses can go along the same network path, because Internet envelopes are sorted again and again—just like post office mail—by special computers along the way. The information (message or data) ends up at the computer to which it was addressed.

What Do Dots Have to Do with It?

The address is the key. Though many individuals and businesses and governments and schools use the Internet, no two users have the same address. These addresses are typical for an individual Internet user:

alice@acsworld.net   rsims@posey.com
cord@ucl.acs.edu   nicky@ecs.co.uk

The Internet user's name is to the left of the @ sign. At the right, dots separate the addresses into levels, called *domains*. In the U.S., the last domain tells the sort of organization it is (**.com** = commercial, **.edu** = education,

- discuss a project with an expert
- send your resume to an employer
- research your genealogy (family history)
- send a birthday card that plays music
- send virtual roses or order real ones
- download (transfer to your computer) a poem
- find good places to go on vacation

.gov = government, .mil = military, .net = network, .org = nonprofit organization) or what country it is in (for example, au = Australia, ca = Canada, ch = Switzerland, mx = Mexico, uk = United Kingdom). All parts to the right of the @ sign further identify the user's domain to send the information to him or her. Many Internet addresses have more dots—more domains—than these examples.

What's E-mail?

Electronic mail, or e-mail, is the first and still most popular use of the Internet. E-mail involves posting (sending) messages (posts) in text form from one computer to another over a network. Speed is the e-mail advantage. A first-class letter takes three to five days going from one coast to the other; even "overnight" mail takes 18 to 24 hours. E-mail posted at 3:45 may arrive on the other side of the country or halfway around the world by 3:46. Delivery in less than five minutes is routine.

Besides posting to individuals, with e-mail you can join discussion (mailing) lists and announcement lists and subscribe to electronic newsletters and magazines (e-zines).

Discussion lists (and similar services: news groups, chat rooms, and forums) center around a topic. Everyone who joins the list is interested in that topic. For example, 125 Vietnam veterans belong to the VWAR-L discussion list. When one member posts a message, all other members receive it and may reply to it. Announcement lists are one-way mailing lists. You can receive messages, but you cannot reply. For example, you might join Monster Board's Job Opportunities announcement list.

Most newsletters and e-zines are text-only e-mail— no fancy type and no glitzy graphics. The low cost of electronic publications allows information to be released sooner and more often than through printed publications.

Is World Wide Web Another Name for the 'Net?

The World Wide Web (the Web) is the main system for navigating (moving from place to place) on the Internet. It lets graphics, audio, and video travel the network paths along with text. Special software called a Web browser allows you to view these sights and sounds and click on links that take you at once to related information in another place. Thus, you can just point and click to navigate the Web.

Microsoft Internet Explorer and Netscape are the most common browsers today. A link that you click is more precisely called a **hyperlink** or **hypertext**—a word or phrase in a different color than surrounding text or underlined. A Web browser opens to a *start page* that contains no information—just dozens of hyperlinks for jumping to other informative or fun places.

How Do You Navigate?

The places that you navigate to are called Web sites, or Web pages, or home pages. (All three names mean the same.) When you click a hyperlink, you may jump—without knowing it—from a Web site in Indiana to one in Indonesia. A few more clicks and you may land on a home page in Ireland. When you find a Web page that you like, you can enter it in your browser and go back to it for updates of the information.

Hyperlinks are not the only way to navigate the Web, though. Every Web site has an address, called a URL (**U**niversal **R**esource **L**ocator). A user can get to a Web site by typing the URL in the browser's Location list box. A URL has domain names like an e-mail address. An example of a URL would be **http://www.bluemountain.com/index.html**. This URL points to the WWW computer at a business named Blue Mountain in the Commercial domain. The http (**H**yper**T**ext **T**ransfer **P**rotocol) refers to the computer language used to get into that computer. The html (**H**yper**T**ext **M**arkup **L**anguage) stands for the programming language used to create all Web pages. (Some word processing applications have add-ons that let users create their own Web pages without knowing HTML.) The browser keeps a list of the URLs used most recently. A user can return to a site another day by clicking its URL on this list instead of typing it again.

Another way to navigate the Web is to use the browser's *search page*. You would use a search page to find information about a certain topic when you don't have a specific URL. On the search page you would type *keywords* to define your search (name the topics and subtopics you want) and select a *search engine* (tool that searches many Web sites to look for your keywords and show you the search results). Common search engines are Alta Vista, InfoSeek, Lycos, and Web Crawler; but there are others.

Whether you jump to a useful or fun site by clicking a hyperlink, go to it directly by typing a URL, or search for it using keywords, you should keep track of it so that you can go to it easily another time. Browsers give you an easy way to do so. In Internet Explorer you add the site to a list of Favorites. In Netscape you attach a Bookmark. All you do is click to capture the site address (URL) and type a name for it. To return to the site, click that name.

The internet continues to change our lives, from how we go to college to how we stay close with cousins. One day you may globe-hop, keying URLs for Web sites in Boise, Bogota, and Bangkok and hyperlinking to Bydogoszcz, Bulawayo, and Berlin—all before lunch. Later, you may seek the advise of a career coach by posting carefully keyed questions to a discussion list; then posting your family's latest news to a few friends from high school. As a keyboard operator with Internet connections, you have the world at your fingertips.

Contents

Contents

Contents

Know Your Hardware

IBM PC or Compatible Computer

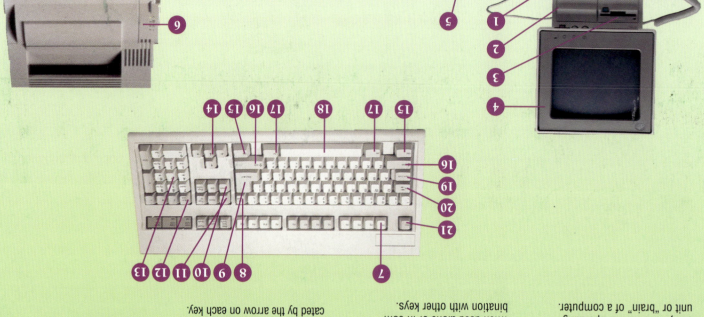

The illustrations below show the major parts of an IBM PC and the keyboard arrangement. The following copy identifies each numbered part.

These parts are found on almost all computers, but their locations may vary. If you are using an IBM PC or compatible computer other than the model illustrated, see the manufacturer's user's guide for the exact location of each part.

Computer and Printer

1. **Keyboard:** an arrangement of letter, figure, symbol, control, function, and editing keys and a numeric keypad.
2. **CPU (Central Processing Unit):** the internal operating unit or "brain" of a computer.
3. **Disk drive:** a unit in or connected to a computer that reads stored data from and writes data to disks (magnetic or optical) for storage.
4. **Monitor:** a TV-like device used to display information on a screen.
5. **Mouse:** a device that is moved across a pad on the desk surface to control movements of a pointer on the screen.
6. **Printer:** a unit connected to a computer that prints copy on paper.

Keyboard Arrangement

7. **Function (F) keys:** perform particular software operations when used alone or in combination with other keys.
8. **Backspace:** deletes the character to the left of the insertion point.
9. **Enter:** causes the insertion point to move to the left margin and down to the next line.
10. **Delete:** deletes the character to the right of the insertion point.
11. **Insert:** switches between insert mode and typeover mode.
12. **Num Lock:** switches the numeric keypad on and off.
13. **Numeric keypad:** a calculator-type keyboard used to enter all-number copy and perform calculations.
14. **Arrow keys:** move the insertion point in the direction indicated by the arrow on each key.
15. **Control (CTRL):** performs a specific software operation when depressed as another key is struck.
16. **Shift key:** makes capital letters and certain symbols when used with those keys.
17. **Alternate (ALT):** performs a specific software command when depressed immediately before or as another key is struck.
18. **Space bar:** inserts space between words and sentences.
19. **Caps Lock:** capitalizes all letters when locked down.
20. **Tab:** moves the insertion point to a preset position.
21. **Escape (ESC):** "backs out" of commands.

Macintosh

The illustrations below show the major parts of a Macintosh computer and the keyboard arrangement. The following copy identifies each numbered part.

These parts are found on almost all computers, but their location may vary. If you are using a Macintosh computer other than the model illustrated, see the manufacturer's user's guide for the exact location of each part.

Computer and Printer

1. **Keyboard:** an arrangement of letter, figure, symbol, control, function, and editing keys and a numeric keypad.
2. **CPU (Central Processing Unit):** the internal operating unit or "brain" of a computer.

3. **Disk drive:** a unit in or connected to a computer that reads stored data from and writes data to disks (magnetic or optical) for storage.
4. **Monitor:** a TV-like device used to display information on a screen.
5. **Mouse:** a device that is moved across a pad on the desk surface to control movements of an indicator on the screen.
6. **Printer:** a unit connected to a computer that prints information on paper.

Keyboard Arrangement

7. **Function (F) keys:** perform particular software operations

when used alone or in combination with other keys.
8. **Delete:** deletes the character to the left of the insertion point.
9. **Return:** causes the insertion point to move to the left margin and down to the next line.
10. **Del:** deletes the character at the insertion point.
11. **Num Lock:** switches the numeric keypad on and off.
12. **Numeric keypad:** a calculator-type keyboard used to enter all-number copy and perform calculations.
13. **Arrow keys:** move the insertion point in the direction indicated by the arrow on each key.

14. **Control:** performs a specific software operation when depressed while another key is struck.
15. **Shift key:** makes capital letters and certain symbols when used with those keys.
16. **⌘ (Command):** performs a specific software command when depressed with another key; menu alternative.
17. **Space bar:** inserts space between words and sentences.
18. **Caps Lock:** capitalizes all letters when locked down.
19. **Tab:** moves the insertion point to a preset position.
20. **Escape (ESC):** "backs out" of commands.

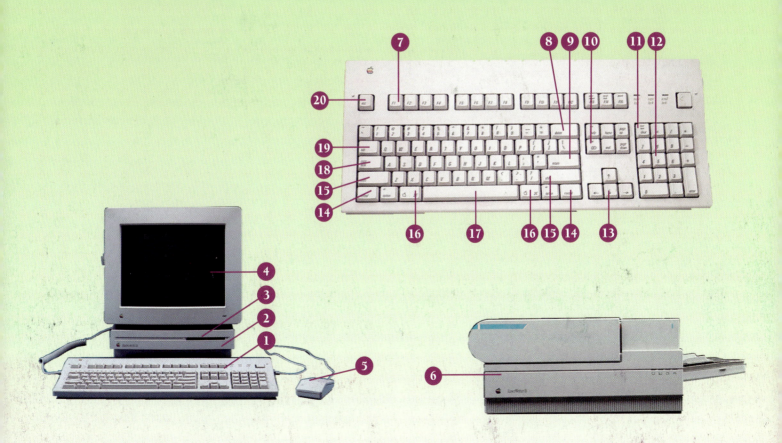

Before you get ready to key, you need to know a few things about *Windows 95*, your computer's operating system software. *Windows 95* also controls the operation of peripherals, such as the mouse and printer hooked up to your computer. All programs that run under *Windows*—for example, *MicroType*, special keyboarding software, and *Microsoft Word* and *WordPerfect*, much-used word processing software—have features in common. (*MicroType*, *Word*, and *WordPerfect* are called application software. An application program enables you to do certain kinds of work, such as writing, editing, and printing a term paper or other report at the computer.) All *Windows* applications have similar buttons; and the menus are much alike, too. Once you learn the basics of *Windows*, you can use that knowledge in every *Windows* application.

Desktop

The opening screen of *Windows 95* simulates a desktop. The small symbols, called icons, on the screen represent items on a desk. Your screen may have other icons besides those listed below.

My Computer displays the disk drives, CD-ROM drive, and printers that are attached to the computer.

Network Neighborhood allows you to view the available resources if you are connected to a network environment.

Recycle Bin stores files that have been deleted from the hard drive. Files deleted in error can be retrieved and put back into their folders. When the recycle bin is emptied, though, the files are gone.

Start displays the Start menu. From the Start menu, you can open a program, open Help, change system settings, close and exit *Windows 95*, and more.

Mouse

Windows software requires the use of a mouse or other pointing device. The mouse is used to select items, to find and move files, and to carry out or cancel commands. The mouse pointer looks different depending on where it is on the screen and what it is doing.

The I-beam shows that the mouse is in the text area of an application. When you pause, it blinks. As you use your application, most of the time you will see the I-beam.

The arrow selects items. It appears when the mouse is outside the text area.

The hourglass shows that *Windows* is processing a command. You must wait until the hourglass disappears before keying text or entering another command.

Move the mouse on a flat, padded surface. If you run out of space, pick up the mouse and put it in another spot. The mouse is used to perform the following actions.

Point: Move the mouse so that the pointer touches a button or text (the words you key).

Click: Point to the desired menu item or button; then press and release the left mouse button once.

Double-click: Point to the desired item and quickly press and release the left mouse button twice.

Click with the right mouse button: Press and release the right mouse button once. A shortcut, or "pop-up," menu appears.

Drag: Point to the desired item; hold down the left mouse button; drag the item to a new location; then release the button.

Taskbar

The strip across the bottom of the computer screen is called the *taskbar*. When *Windows 95* is running, the Start button shows on the taskbar (Figure 1). When you click Start, a menu displays with the commands for using *Windows 95* (Figure 2). The commands you will likely use most are Programs and Shut Down. Each time you open a program, a button with the name of that program appears on the taskbar, beside the Start button. The taskbar in Figure 1 shows that *Microsoft Word* is open.

Taskbar

Start

Figure 1: *Windows 95* Opening Screen

Figure 2: Start Menu

Programs

When you click the Programs command (Start menu), another menu displays. This menu shows the names of *Windows 95* applications installed on your computer (Figure 3). On this menu, the word *Accessories* stands for a group of applications built into *Windows 95* (Figure 4). (Other applications are installed separately, not built-in.) A *Windows* accessory that you may use with this book is the calculator (Figure 5).

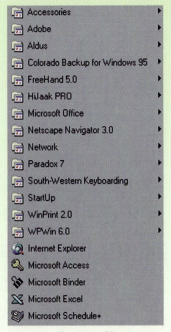

Figure 3: Program Menu

Figure 4: Accessories Menu

Figure 5: *Windows* Calculator Accessory

If *MicroType Pro* or *MicroType Multimedia* has been installed, you will see it on the Programs menu. When you double-click the icon beside the name of this application, the software will open and a *MicroType* button will appear on the taskbar.

If you will be using word processing software such as *Microsoft Word* or *WordPerfect* instead of *MicroType Pro*, you should find the word processing application on the Programs menu. Clicking its icon will open it and add its button to the taskbar. Once the software opens, you can see the following features (Figure 6) that all *Windows 95* applications have in common.

Minimize, Restore, and Close buttons: Clicking the Minimize button reduces the application to an icon. Clicking the icon (on the taskbar) restores the application to full size. The Restore button makes a full-size application smaller and makes a small one full size. The Close button exits the application and removes its icon from the taskbar. Within the application, each document window (where you type) also has Minimize, Restore, and Close buttons.

Menu bar: Clicking any word on the Menu bar displays a drop-down menu. Arrows indicate sub-menus.

Scroll bars: Clicking an arrow on a scroll bar moves the window in the direction of the arrow—up or down and left or right.

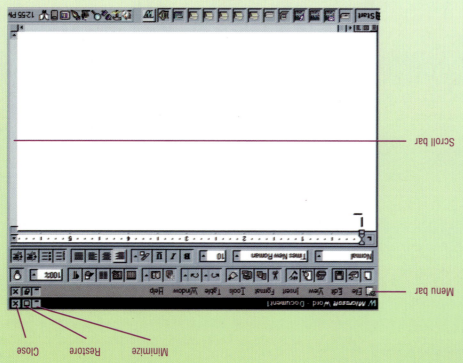

Close
Restore
Minimize

Menu bar

Scroll bar

Figure 6: A *Windows 95* Application

With *MicroType Pro* or *MicroType Multimedia*, you can use the power of your computer to learn alphabetic and numeric keyboarding and keypad operation. After you do Lesson 14, you can use Keyboarding Skill Builder to boost speed and to improve accuracy. Almost any time, you can go to *MicroType's* Open Screen—a simple word processor—to master new keys, practice techniques, or take timed writings. **Suggestion:** Use the Open Screen for parts D and E of the Reviews and all of Lessons 16, 17, 23, 24, 29, and 30. The Open Screen also may be used for the word processing applications on pp. A1-A8.

Alphabetic Keyboarding

The Alphabetic Keyboarding lessons present the letter keys and basic punctuation keys (two keys per lesson). Lesson numbers in the software and book are not the same, but keys are presented in the same order. **Suggestion:** After doing a lesson in the book, do the software lesson that presents the same new keys. *MicroType* offers varied keyboard activities, including an occasional game. It uses typing modes with names like "word-lock," "lock-and-flash," and "line-check."

Numeric Keyboarding

Numeric Keyboarding presents the figure keys and 12 symbols/punctuation keys (two per lesson). The suggestion above works here, too. **Note:** *MicroType Pro* does not have a lesson to go with Lesson 28; this lesson is in *MicroType Multimedia*, however.

Numeric Keypad

The four Numeric Keypad lessons in *MicroType* match the Numeric Keypad supplement on pp. 77-80. The software sums the figures you enter so that you can check your work for accuracy. The work is designed to help you become fast (speed is measured in *kspm*, or keystrokes per minute) as well as accurate on the keypad.

Open Screen Timer

MicroType's Open Screen has a Count-Down Timer that is well suited for the timings called for in this book. You set the timer. When you start to type, it starts to count down from the time you set until it reaches zero. You can set it for the many one-minute writings in this book and the three-minute writings used to assess your skill. You can select the Variable option to do longer or shorter writings. **Suggestion:** Build skill (practice) with frequent short timings (20 seconds to one minute); measure skill with occasional longer timings (two to three minutes). This idea is built into the directions in this book.

For the dozen *guided writings* in this book, you set a speed goal and set the timer for one minute. To reach your goal, though, you need feedback every few seconds to know whether to speed up or slow down. *MicroType* can do that: You can choose to have the timer beep or flash every 15 seconds during a longer writing.

Minimum System Requirements

To run *MicroType Pro* for *Windows* (0-538-66201-8), you need an IBM® Compatible Personal Computer with a 386 /33MHz microprocessor or higher, 4 MB RAM (8 MB recommended), a 40 MB hard drive with 9 MB free, a high-density 3.5" floppy drive, a monitor with 640x480 display resolution with 256 colors (Super VGA), a 101-key keyboard, and a mouse. A Sound-Blaster compatible sound card is optional. *MicroType Pro* is compatible with *Microsoft Windows 95, Windows 3.1, MS-DOS,* or *PC-DOS 3.3* or higher; also, *Novell networks* and *ICLAS* systems.

To run *MicroType Pro* for Macintosh (0-538-66202-6), you need an Apple Macintosh® Personal Computer with a 16MHz 68030 microprocessor or higher, 4 MB RAM (8 MB recommended), a 40 MB hard drive with 8 MB free, a high-density 3.5" floppy drive, a color monitor with 640x480 display resolution with 256 colors, standard internal Macintosh audio, an Apple Keyboard II or equivalent, a mouse, and an Apple System 7.0 or higher. *MicroType Pro* for Macintosh is compatible with *AppleShare* and *AppleTalk* networks.

Questions? For more information about *MicroType Pro* or *MicroType MultiMedia* (1998 release), call 1-800-824-5179 or visit South-Western's Web site at http://www.swep.com.

To place an order. To order *MicroType Pro* or *MicroType MultiMedia,* call 1-800-354-9706 or visit http://www.swep.com on the Web.

Turn On the Operating System (Start Windows 95)

Become familiar with the steps for turning on your computer equipment. Do the steps in the same order every time.

1. If a disk is in the disk drive, remove it.
2. If a printer will be used, turn on its power switch.
3. Turn on the power switch on the CPU (and monitor if it has a separate switch). The *Windows 95* screen will display.
4. If the *Windows 95* screen contains a tip, read the tip and click the Close button.

Open the Word Processing Program

Your word processing program, or application, may open automatically when *Windows 95* opens (if the program is in the StartUp group). If not, then you must open the word processing software.

1. Click the Start button on the taskbar (lower left corner of screen).
2. On the Start menu, point to the Programs command.
3. On the drop-down menu, find the name of your word processing application, and click the icon beside the name. The word processing program opens and its button shows on the taskbar.

Do Basic Word Processing Operations

Using a word processing application involves creating, saving, closing, opening, and printing documents. (Anything that you type in the text area is a *document*. Another word for document is *file*.) These five operations are not all that you can do on word processing software—just the most basic operations. You need nothing more than the character keys (and space bar) on your keyboard to create a document. To save, close, open, and print, though, you need to access the function in one of three ways: (1) click a button on the Power bar or Toolbar; (2) use a keyboard command; or (3) select an option from a pull-down menu on the Menu bar.

Power bar/Toolbar. A Power bar or Toolbar is a series of buttons, or icons. See the illustrations at the top of this page. On both bars, the second, third, and fourth buttons from the left stand for Open (an open folder), Save (a disk), and Print (a printer). To use a function, click its button.

Keyboard commands. Many word processing operations, including save, close, open, and print, can be done with keyboard commands. The commands may be an F (function) key (for example, F5) or a combination of Ctrl or Alt and another key (an F key or letter key). The keyboard commands are shown on the pull-down menus. On the Corel® WordPerfect® File menu, for example, you see that the keyboard command to open a file is Ctrl+O; the command to close a file is Ctrl+F4. On the Microsoft *Word* File menu, Ctrl+S is the keyboard command to save a file, Ctrl+P to print. The easiest commands to remember are the ones—like Open (Ctrl+O) and Save (Ctrl+S)—that combine Ctrl and the first letter of the function.

Microsoft Word Toolbar

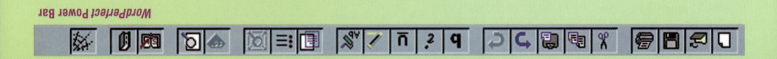

WordPerfect Power Bar

Know Word Processing Software

Pull-down menus. A pull-down menu may be used to choose word processing operations. For the basic operations, pull down (click) the File menu on the Menu bar (upper left corner). Then, click the option you want.

WordPerfect **File Menu**

Microsoft Word **File Menu**

Create a Document (File)

The I-beam (mouse pointer) blinks in the text area. It is the *insertion point.* If you strike a character (letter, figure, or symbol) key, the character appears in that spot; and the insertion point moves to the right, ready for another character. The line spacing on the word processing application is preset for single spacing. The top, bottom, and side margins are preset at 1" in most cases. These settings are called *defaults.* Of course you may use the default line spacing and margins, but you also may choose to change these settings.

Set line spacing. With single spacing (1.0) being the default setting, one-and-a-half spacing (1.5) and double spacing (2.0) are common choices. Most word processing applications offer many more line-spacing options (1.12, 1.75, 2.5, 4, etc.).

1. Place the insertion point (click the I-beam) where you want the line spacing to change. (In some software, line spacing will change for the entire paragraph in which the insertion point is placed.)

2. Select the option to change line spacing, using the proper Power bar/Toolbar button, pull-down menu, or keyboard command.

3. Specify the line spacing you want.

4. Begin or continue keying.

Set margins. If you want to change the default margins, specify a different setting for the margin(s) you want changed.

1. Place the insertion point (click the I-beam) where the margin setting is to be changed (at beginning or anywhere within a document).

2. Select the option that changes margins, using the proper Power bar/Toolbar button, pull-down menu, or keyboard command.

3. Specify the new setting(s).

4. Begin or continue keying. To change margins back to the default settings, repeat these steps.

Save a Document (File)

When you save a file, you place a copy of it on a disk in one of the computer's disk drives, while leaving a copy of it on the screen. To save a document not saved before, you must give it a name (filename). A document may be saved before you key any text, while you are working, or when you are done working.

1. Select the Save option, using the proper Power bar/Toolbar button, pull-down menu, or keyboard command. (The Save As box will display if the file has not been saved before.)

2. Choose where (which disk drive and/or directory or folder) you want to save the file.

3. Assign a filename that will help you find the file whenever you want to open it later. Check the software user's guide for how many letters you may use in a filename. **Note:** Newer software accepts filenames that have over two hundred characters, but some applications limit filenames to eight characters.

4. Begin or continue keying; or, if you are done working, close the file.

5. If you modify (change) this file and want to save the modified file, select the Save option, using the proper Power bar/Toolbar button, pull-down menu, or keyboard command. To keep the original document and the modified document in separate files, select the Save As option, using the proper Power bar/Toolbar button, pull-down menu, or keyboard command.

Close a Document (File)

When you close a file, you remove it from the screen. If the copy on the screen has not been saved, or if it has been changed since it was last saved, you will be asked if you want to save the document before closing it.

1. Select the option that closes a file, using the proper Power bar/Toolbar button, pull-down menu, or keyboard command. **Note:** If you are running *Windows 95*, click the X button at the far right on the Menu bar to close a file. Be careful; clicking the large X in the upper right corner will close your word processing software.

2. If the *Save changes . . . ?* prompt comes on the screen, click Yes to save changes you have made in the original file. Click No to close the document without saving changes.

Open a Document (File)

When you open a file, you retrieve it from the disk drive and directory and/or folder in which you saved it. An open file appears in the text area.

1. Choose the correct disk drive, if necessary. **Note:** Disk drives are named with letters of the alphabet. In most cases, the main disk drive inside the computer is the c-drive (c:\). It is the default drive, which means that you do not have to choose a disk drive to open files saved on this drive. The drive that takes floppy (square plastic) disks is usually the a-drive (a:\). The drive that reads CD-ROM (round silver) disks may be the d-drive (d:\) or another letter.

2. Select the option that lets you see a list of items saved on the disk you chose. Use the proper Power bar/Toolbar button, pull-down menu, or keyboard command.

3. If you saved the file in a subdirectory or folder, open (click) the subdirectory or folder; then select the file you want to open.

Print a Document (File)

When you print a document, you send a copy of it to a printer that can make a paper (hard) copy of the file.

1. If more than one printer is available, be sure that the printer you want to use is selected in the software. **Note:** The File menu may have an option just for selecting a printer. If not, select the printer in Step 2, after selecting the print option.

2. Select the print option, using the proper Power bar/Toolbar button, pull-down menu, or keyboard command. **Note:** On some software, clicking the Power bar/Toolbar Print button may print *all* pages of a document automatically. If you want to print only one page or selected pages, use Print on the pull-down menu or use the keyboard command. (The *current page* is the page that has the insertion point in it.) To print selected pages, type a range of pages (example: 2-5) or specific pages (example: 1,4,5).

3. Take your printed page(s) from the printer.

Turn off the Operating System (Shut Down)

The Shut Down command (Start menu) is used to close the *Windows 95* operating system. (Most computer users shut down after using the computer for the last time each day, not at the end of each session.)

1. Close the open files on your application software.

2. If a floppy disk is in the disk drive, remove it.

3. Click Shut Down on the Start menu.

4. Select (Click) Yes at the *Shut down computer?* prompt. Your word processing software will close.

5. Wait for this prompt: *It's now safe to turn off your computer.*

6. Turn off the power switch on the CPU (and monitor if it has a separate switch).

Learn Letter Keyboarding Technique

Lesson 1   Home Keys (FDSA JKL;)

O b j e c t i v e s :

1. To learn control of home keys (FDSA JKL;).
2. To learn control of Space Bar and Return/Enter.

1 A ◆

Work Area

Arrange work area as shown at right.

- alphanumeric (main) keyboard directly in front of chair; front edge of keyboard even with edge of table or desk
- monitor placed for easy viewing; disk drives placed for easy access
- your word processing disks within easy reach
- *MicroType Pro* disks or *MicroType Multimedia* CD within reach (if available); see p. xiii
- book behind or at right of keyboard, resting on easel for easy reading

Properly arranged work area

1 B ◆

Keying Position

The essential features of proper position are shown at right and listed below:

- fingers curved and upright over home keys
- wrists low, but not touching frame of keyboard
- forearms parallel to slant of keyboard
- body erect; sitting back in chair
- feet on floor for balance

Proper position at computer

Proper position at computer

Section C

New Keys: 1/2/3

Objectives:
1. To learn reach-strokes for 1, 2, and 3.
2. To combine quickly the new keys with other keys learned.

C1 ◆ 5
Keypad Review

Enter the columns of data listed at the right as directed in Steps 1-5 on p. 78.

A	B	C	D	E	F	G
44	74	740	996	704	990	477
55	85	850	885	805	880	588
66	96	960	774	906	770	699

C2 ◆ 35
New Keys: 1/2/3

Learn reach to 1
1. Locate 1 (below 4) on the numeric keypad.
2. Watch your index finger move down to 1 and back to 4 a few times *without striking keys*.
3. Practice striking 14 a few times as you watch the finger.
4. Enter the data in Drills 1A and 1B.

Learn reach to 2
1. Learn the middle-finger reach to 2 (below 5) as directed in Steps 1-3 above.
2. Enter data in Drills 1C and 1D.

Learn reach to 3
1. Learn the ring-finger reach to 3 (below 6) as directed above.
2. Enter data in Drills 1E, 1F, and 1G.

Drills 2-4

Enter data in Drills 2-4 until you can do so accurately and quickly.

Drill 1

A	B	C	D	E	F	G
414	141	525	252	636	363	174
141	111	252	222	363	333	285
111	414	222	525	333	636	396

Drill 2

A	B	C	D	E	F	G
114	225	336	175	415	184	174
411	522	633	284	524	276	258
141	252	363	395	635	359	369

Drill 3

A	B	C	D	E	F	G
417	528	639	110	171	471	714
147	280	369	220	282	582	850
174	285	396	330	393	693	936

Drill 4

A	B	C	D	E	F	G
77	71	401	107	417	147	174
88	82	502	208	528	258	825
99	93	603	309	639	369	396

C3 ◆ 10
Numbers with Decimals

Enter the data in Columns A-F, placing the decimals as shown in the copy.

A	B	C	D	E	F
1.40	17.10	47.17	174.11	1,477.01	10,704.50
2.50	28.20	58.28	285.22	2,588.02	17,815.70
3.60	39.30	69.39	396.33	3,996.03	20,808.75
4.70	74.70	17.10	417.14	4,174.07	26,909.65
5.80	85.80	28.20	528.25	5,285.08	30,906.25
6.90	96.90	39.30	639.36	6,396.06	34,259.90

1C ◆

Home-Key Position

1. Find the home keys on the chart: **F D S A** for left hand and **J K L ;** for right hand.
2. Locate the home keys on your keyboard. Place left-hand fingers on **F D S A** and right-hand fingers on **J K L ;** *with your fingers well curved and upright (not slanting).*
3. Remove your fingers from the keyboard; then place them in home-key position again, curving and holding them *lightly* on the keys.

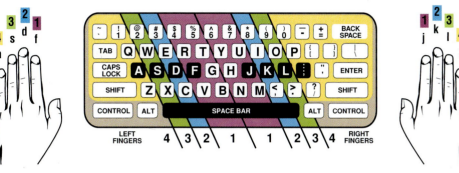

1D ◆

Technique: Home Keys and Space Bar

1. Read the statements and study the illustrations at right.
2. Place your fingers in home-key position as directed in 1C above.
3. Strike each letter key for the first group of letters in the line of type below the technique illustrations.
4. After striking ; (semicolon), strike the **Space Bar** once.
5. Continue to key the line; strike the **Space Bar** once at the point of each arrow.

TECHNIQUE CUES:

Keystroking: Strike each key with a light tap with the tip of the finger, snapping the fingertip toward the palm of the hand.

Spacing: Strike the Space Bar with the right thumb; use a quick down-and-in motion (toward the palm). Avoid pauses before or after spacing.

Light tap with finger tip

Snap finger tip toward palm

Strike Space Bar with right thumb

Quick down-and-in spacing motion

Space once.

fdsajkl; f d s a j k l ; ff jj dd kk ss ll aa ;;

Section B

New Keys: 7/8/9

Objectives:

1. To learn reach-strokes for 7, 8, and 9.
2. To combine quickly the new keys with other keys learned.

B1◆ 5
Home-Key Review

Enter the columns of data listed at the right as directed in Steps 1-5 on p. 78.

A	B	C	D	E	F
4	44	400	404	440	450
5	55	500	505	550	560
6	66	600	606	660	456

B2◆ 45
New Keys: 7/8/9

Learn reach to 7

1. Locate 7 (above 4) on the numeric keypad.
2. Watch your index finger move up to 7 and back to 4 a few times *without striking keys*.
3. Practice striking 74 a few times as you watch the finger.
4. With eyes on copy, enter the data in Drills 1A and 1B.

Learn reach to 8

1. Learn the middle-finger reach to 8 (above 5) as directed in Steps 1-3 above.
2. With eyes on copy, enter the data in Drills 1C and 1D.

Learn reach to 9

1. Learn the ring-finger reach to 9 (above 6) as directed above.
2. With eyes on copy, enter the data in Drills 1E and 1F.

Drills 2-4

Practice entering the columns of data in Drills 2-4 until you can do so accurately and quickly.

Drill 1

A	B	C	D	E	F
474	747	585	858	696	969
747	777	858	888	969	999
777	474	888	585	999	696

Drill 2

A	B	C	D	E	F
774	885	996	745	475	754
474	585	696	854	584	846
747	858	969	965	695	956

Drill 3

A	B	C	D	E	F
470	580	690	770	707	407
740	850	960	880	808	508
704	805	906	990	909	609

Drill 4

A	B	C	D	E	F
456	407	508	609	804	905
789	408	509	704	805	906
654	409	607	705	806	907
987	507	608	706	904	908

Enrichment

Windows Calculator Accessory

Enter single, double, and triple digits as shown, striking + between numbers. Clear the total after each drill.

A	B	C	D	E	F
4	90	79	4	740	860
56	87	64	56	64	70
78	68	97	78	960	900
90	54	64	60	89	67
4	6	5	98	8	80

1E ◆
Technique: Hard Return at Line Endings

To return the insertion point to left margin and move it down to next line, strike **Return/Enter** key (hard return).

Study illustration at right; then return 4 times (quadruple-space) below the line you completed in 1D, p. 2.

Hard Return

Striking the **Enter** (IBM or compatible) or **Return** (Macintosh)

key is called a *hard return.* You will use a hard return at the end of all drill lines in this lesson and those that follow in this unit. Reach the little finger of the right hand to the **Enter** or **Return** key, tap the key, and return the finger quickly to home-key position.

1F ◆
Home-Key and Space Bar Practice

1. Place your hands in home-key position (left-hand fingers on **F D S A** and right-hand fingers on **J K L** ;).
2. Key the lines once: single-spaced (SS) with a double space (DS) between 2-line groups. Do not key line numbers.

Fingers curved and upright

Down-and-in spacing motion

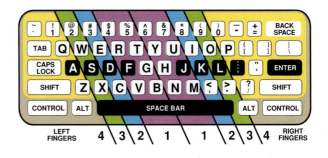

LEFT FINGERS 4 3 2 1   1 2 3 4 RIGHT FINGERS

Strike Space Bar once to space.

```
1  j  jj  f  ff  k  kk  d  dd  l  ll  s  ss  ;  ;;  a  aa  jkl;  fdsa
2  j  jj  f  ff  k  kk  d  dd  l  ll  s  ss  ;  ;;  a  aa  jkl;  fdsa
```
Strike the Return/Enter key twice to double-space (DS).

```
3  a  aa  ;  ;;  s  ss  l  ll  d  dd  k  kk  f  ff  j  jj  fdsa  jkl;
4  a  aa  ;  ;;  s  ss  l  ll  d  dd  k  kk  f  ff  j  jj  fdsa  jkl;
```
DS

```
5  jf  jf  kd  kd  ls  ls  ;a  ;a  fj  fj  dk  dk  sl  sl  a;  a;  f
6  jf  jf  kd  kd  ls  ls  ;a  ;a  fj  fj  dk  dk  sl  sl  a;  a;  f
```
DS

```
7  a;fj  a;sldkfj  a;sldkfj  a;sldkfj  a;sldkfj  a;sldkfj
8  a;fj  a;sldkfj  a;sldkfj  a;sldkfj  a;sldkfj  a;sldkfj
```
Strike the Return/Enter key 4 times to quadruple-space (QS).

1G ◆
Technique: Return

each line twice single-spaced (SS); double-space (DS) between 2-line groups

SPACING CUE:

When in SS mode, strike **Return/Enter** twice to insert a DS between 2-line groups.

Reach out with little finger; tap **Return/Enter** key quickly; return finger to home key.

```
1  a;sldkfj  a;sldkfj
```
DS

```
2  ff  jj  dd  kk  ss  ll  aa  ;;
```
DS

```
3  fj  fj  dk  dk  sl  sl  a;  a;  asdf  ;lkj
```
DS

```
4  fj  dk  sl  a;  jf  kd  ls  ;a  fdsa  jkl;  a;sldkfj
```
QS

A3◆ 40

New Keys: 4/5/6/0 (Home Keys)

Complete the drills as directed below. If you are using word processing software (instead of the Numeric Keypad section of *Micro-Type*), enter the numbers in one continuous column. The screen will fill quickly because numbers are listed vertically. Therefore, clear the screen after each drill.

1. Curve the fingers of your right hand; place them upright on the home keys:
   - index finger on 4
   - middle finger on 5
   - ring finger on 6
   - thumb on 0
2. Using the special Enter key (at right of keypad), enter data in Drill 1A as follows:
   - 4 Enter
   - 4 Enter
   - 4 Enter
   - Strike Enter
3. Enter Columns 1B-1F in the same way.
4. Using the special Enter key, enter data in Drill 2A as follows:
   - 44 Enter
   - 44 Enter
   - 44 Enter
   - Strike Enter
5. Continue Drill 2 and complete Drills 3-5 in a similar way. In Drills 4 and 5, strike 0 with side of right thumb.

When you can operate the keypad by touch—all drills completed through p. 80—open the Windows calculator accessory. Key Drill 1A at the right, striking the + key between numbers. Clear the calculator screen (click C); then rekey Drill 1A. Key each remaining drill twice. If the two totals of a single drill are not the same, key the drill a third time at a slower pace.

TECHNIQUE CUE:
Strike each key with a quick, sharp stroke with the *tip* of the finger; release the key quickly. Keep the fingers curved and upright; the wrist low, relaxed, and steady.

Drill 1

A	B	C	D	E	F
4	5	6	4	5	6
4	5	6	4	5	6
4	5	6	4	5	6

Drill 2

A	B	C	D	E	F
44	55	66	44	55	66
44	55	66	44	55	66
44	55	66	44	55	66

Drill 3

A	B	C	D	E	F
44	45	54	44	55	66
55	56	46	45	54	65
66	64	65	46	56	64

Drill 4

A	B	C	D	E	F
40	50	60	400	500	600
40	50	60	400	500	600
40	50	60	400	500	600

Drill 5

A	B	C	D	E	F
40	400	404	406	450	650
50	500	505	506	540	560
60	600	606	606	405	605

1H◆
Home-Key Mastery

1. Key the lines once (without the numbers); strike the **Return/Enter** key twice to double-space (DS).
2. Rekey the drill at a faster pace.

TECHNIQUE CUE:
Keep fingers curved and upright over home keys, right thumb just barely touching the Space Bar.

SPACING CUE:
Space once after ; used as punctuation.

Correct finger alignment

1 aa ;; ss ll dd kk ff jj a; sl dk fj jf kd ls ;a jf
DS

2 a a as as ad ad ask ask lad lad fad fad jak jak la
DS

3 all all fad fad jak jak add add ask ask ads ads as
DS

4 a lad; a jak; a lass; all ads; add all; ask a lass
DS

5 as a lad; a fall fad; ask all dads; as a fall fad;

1I◆
End-of-Lesson Routine

1. Exit the software.
2. Remove from disk drive any disk you have inserted.
3. Store materials.

Disk removal

Most computer manufacturers recommend turning a computer off at the end of the day, rather than immediately after each use.

Enrichment

1. Key drill once as shown to improve control of home keys.
2. Key the drill again to quicken your keystrokes.

SPACING CUE:
To DS when in SS mode, strike **Return/Enter** twice at end of line.

1 ja js jd jf f; fl fk fj ka ks kd kf d; dl dk dj a;
DS

2 la ls ld lf s; sl sk sj ;a ;s ;d ;f a; al ak aj fj
DS

3 jj aa kk ss ll dd ;; ff fj dk sl a; jf kd ls ;a a;
DS

4 as as ask ask ad ad lad lad all all fall fall lass
DS

5 as a fad; as a dad; ask a lad; as a lass; all lads
DS

6 a sad dad; all lads fall; ask a lass; a jak salad;
DS

7 add a jak; a fall ad; all fall ads; ask a sad lass

Lesson 1

Section A

New Keys: 4/5/6/0

Objectives:
1. To learn reach-strokes for 4, 5, 6, and 0.
2. To key these home-key numbers with speed and ease.

A1 ◆ 5

Numeric Keypad Arrangement

Figure keys 1-9 are in standard locations on numeric keypads.

The zero (0) key location may vary slightly from one keyboard to another.

The illustrations at the right show the location of the numeric keypad on selected computer keyboards.

> Use Numeric Keypad in *MicroType* to follow up Section A, B, and C.

Macintosh LCII numeric keypad

IBM PC numeric keypad

A2 ◆ 5

Operating Position

1. Position yourself in front of the keyboard—body erect, both feet on floor for balance.
2. Place this book, resting on easel, for easy reading—at right of keyboard or directly behind it.
3. Curve the fingers of the right hand and place them on the keypad:
   - index finger on 4
   - middle finger on 5
   - ring finger on 6
   - thumb on 0

> To use the keypad, the Num (number) Lock must be turned on.

Book at right of keyboard

Proper position at keyboard

Review

Objectives:

1. **To improve control of the home keys (FDSA JKL:).**
2. **To improve control of Space Bar and Return/Enter.**

RA◆
Get Ready to Key

1. Arrange your work area (see p. 1).
2. Get to know your hardware and software (see pp. viii-xvi).
3. Use default margins and spacing. The word **default** refers to margins and spacing that the software chooses, rather than choices you indicate.
4. Take keying position as shown at right.

RB◆
Home-Key Position

1. Locate the home keys on the chart: **F D S A** for left hand and **J K L ;** for right hand.
2. Locate the home keys on your keyboard. Place left-hand fingers on **F D S A** and right-hand fingers on **J K L ;** *with fingers well curved and upright (not slanting).*
3. Remove fingers from the keyboard; then place them in home-key position again.

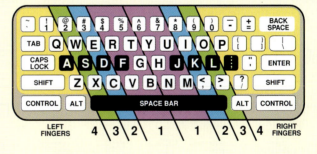

RC◆
Technique Review

Remember to use a hard return at the end of all drill lines. To double-space (DS), use two hard returns again.

Keystroke
Curve fingers over home keys. Strike each key with a quick-snap stroke; release key quickly.

Space
Strike the **Space Bar** with a quick down-and-in motion of the right thumb. Do not pause before or after spacing stroke.

Hard Return
Reach the right little finger to the **Return/Enter** key; strike the key and return the finger quickly to home key.

30C◆ 15
Skill Assessment: Straight Copy

1. Key a 1' writing on ¶ 1; find *gwam*.
2. Key a 1' *guided* writing on the ¶, trying to reach your checkpoint each 1/4'. (See p. 45 if needed.)
3. Key ¶ 2 in the same manner.
4. Key two 2' writings on ¶s 1-2 combined; find *gwam* on each.
5. Key two 3' writings on ¶s 1-2 combined; find *gwam*, count errors on each.

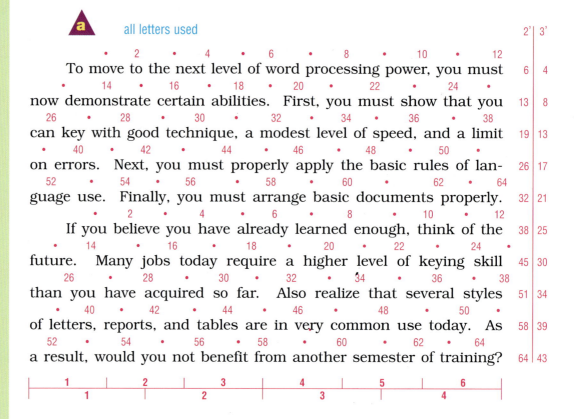

a all letters used

	2'	3'
To move to the next level of word processing power, you must	6	4
now demonstrate certain abilities. First, you must show that you	13	8
can key with good technique, a modest level of speed, and a limit	19	13
on errors. Next, you must properly apply the basic rules of lan-	26	17
guage use. Finally, you must arrange basic documents properly.	32	21
If you believe you have already learned enough, think of the	38	25
future. Many jobs today require a higher level of keying skill	45	30
than you have acquired so far. Also realize that several styles	51	34
of letters, reports, and tables are in very common use today. As	58	39
a result, would you not benefit from another semester of training?	64	43

30D◆ 15
Skill Transfer: Statistical Copy

1. Key three 1' writings on each ¶; find *gwam* on each writing.
2. Key two 3' writings on ¶s 1-2 combined; find *gwam* on each.
3. Compare *gwam* with that attained on ¶s in 30C.
4. Key additional 3' writings on the slower ¶s to improve your skill transfer.

a all figures used

	3'
Since its first showing in 1939, 197.5 million people in the	4 48
USA have attended a theater to see "Gone with the Wind." When its	9 53
gross sales are adjusted for inflation, its $859 million income	13 57
makes it the top-selling film in our history. It exceeds "Star Wars"	17 62
(released in 1977) by $229 million; "E.T." (1982) by $289 million.	22 66
In addition, "The Ten Commandments" (1958) and "The Sound of	26 70
Music" (1965) outsold "Jurassic Park" (1993) and "Return of the Jedi"	31 75
(1983) by a large margin. "Fantasia" (1940) also surpassed "The Empire	35 79
Strikes Back" (1980) and "The Godfather" (1972). The classic film, it	40 84
seems, holds its own against the modern "blockbuster" film.	44 88

RD◆

Home Keys and Space Bar

Key the lines once (without numbers), single-spaced (SS) with a double space between 2-line groups.

Technique goals

- curved, upright fingers
- quick-snap keystrokes
- down-and-in spacing
- quick return without spacing at line endings

Correct finger curvature

Correct finger alignment

Strike Space Bar once to space.

```
1 f ff j jj d dd k kk s ss l ll a aa ; ;; fdsa jkl;
2 f ff j jj d dd k kk s ss l ll a aa ; ;; fdsa jkl;
```
Strike the Return/Enter key twice to double-space (DS).
```
3 j jj f ff k kk d dd l ll s ss ; ;; a aa asdf ;lkj
4 j jj f ff k kk d dd l ll s ss ; ;; a aa asdf ;lkj
                                                  DS
5 a;a sls dkd fjf ;a; lsl kdk jfj a;sldkfj a;sldkfj
6 a;a sls dkd fjf ;a; lsl kdk jfj a;sldkfj a;sldkfj
```
Strike the Return/Enter key 4 times to quadruple-space (QS).

RE◆

Home-Key Stroking

Key the lines single-spaced (SS) with a double space (DS) between 2-line groups. Do not key the line numbers.

Goal

To improve keying and spacing techniques.

```
1 f f ff j j jj d d dd k k kk s s ss l l ll a a aa;;
2 f f ff j j jj d d dd k k kk s s ss l l ll a a aa;;
3 fj dk sl a; jf kd ls ;a ds kl df kj sd lk sa ;l ja
4 fj dk sl a; jf kd ls ;a ds kl df kj sd lk sa ;l ja
5 sa as ld dl af fa ls sl fl lf al la ja aj sk ks ja
6 sa as ld dl af fa ls sl fl lf al la ja aj sk ks ja
```

RF◆

Technique: Return

each line twice single-spaced (SS); double-space (DS) between 2-line groups

Technique goals

- curved, upright fingers
- quick-snap keystrokes
- down-and-in spacing
- quick return without spacing at line endings

TECHNIQUE CUE:

Reach out with the little finger, not the hand; tap **Return/Enter** quickly; return finger to home key.

```
1 a;sldkfj a;sldkfj
                    DS
2 a ad ad a as as ask ask
                          DS
3 as as jak jak ads ads all all
                                DS
4 a jak; a lass; all fall; ask all dads
                                        DS
5 as a fad; add a jak; all fall ads; a sad lass
                                               QS
```

Lesson 30

Skill Assessment

Objectives:
1. To improve/assess keying skill on sentences and paragraphs.
2. To improve skill transfer: straight copy to statistical copy.

30A ◆ 5
Conditioning Practice

1. Key each line once; then key each line again faster.
2. Key a 1' writing on line 3; find *gwam*.

alphabet 1   Jacki next placed my winning bid for the prized antique red vase.

figures 2   717 828 939 417 528 639 707 9.9 407.96 104.39 371.3649 45205-4238

speed 3   They wish their neighbor to pay for half the land for the chapel.

| 1 | 2 | 3 | 4 | 5 | 6 | 7 | 8 | 9 | 10 | 11 | 12 | 13 |

30B ◆ 15
Technique Mastery

1. Key each line once; note lines that cause you to pause or hesitate.
2. Key a 1' writing on each of lines 15, 18, and 21; find *gwam* on each writing.
3. As time permits, key again those sets of lines that caused you to pause or stop.

Technique goals
- curved, upright fingers
- quick-snap keystrokes
- no finger "flyout"
- down-and-in spacing
- eyes on copy

Keep hands/arms quiet; *reach* with the fingers.

shift keys & LOCK
1   LaCosta Spa| Halley's Comet| Palm Springs| Margate Court| Esprit Park
2   Marla Apton and Pat Cox will play Nan Epps and Larry Sparks next.
3   Sophie works in Boston for NBC; Paula works in Nantucket for CBS.

long, direct reaches
4   grip hymn echo many deck must curve funny niece doubt twice brown
5   my niece| ace serve| any doubt| iced juice| sunny deck| my music echos
6   Cecil had much fun at the gym and the new ice center this summer.

outside reaches
7   lop pox zoo spa cape pawn spot oars wasp maps span slow aqua slaw
8   old pal| low spot| all maps| alto sax| slow pace| next quiz| saw a fawn
9   Silas won a prized spot on our next squad that took a town title.

adjacent keys
10   her top saw ore by went open coin spot skew ruin soil trot built
11   her suit| buy gas| new coin| was open| last poem| went well| very short
12   Jeremy was to open a coin shop in a new store in the town square.

double letters
13   mall cuff will soon meek door need seeks books sells peeks little
14   to err| for all| odd book| sell off| zoo pass| too meek| will soon need
15   Ann will take all her old cookbooks to sell at the school bazaar.

combi-nation response
16   sign pump with fear them plum lake were make cafe name join shale
17   and you| for him| man was| pay him| they were| with care| to you or him
18   It was up to you or him to read and amend the audit form by noon.

word response
19   their sight ivory shall flame right amend eight gowns bland girls
20   six girls| ivory gown| their risk| title form| right firm| ivory tusks
21   They may make the amendment to the title form for their neighbor.

| 1 | 2 | 3 | 4 | 5 | 6 | 7 | 8 | 9 | 10 | 11 | 12 | 13 |

RG ◆
Home-Key Mastery

each line twice single-spaced (SS); double-space (DS) between 2-line groups

Technique goals
- curved, upright fingers
- eyes on copy in book or on screen
- quick-snap keystrokes
- down-and-in spacing
- steady pace

Correct finger curvature

Correct finger alignment

Down-and-in spacing motion

```
1 a jak; a jak; ask dad; ask dad; as all; as all ads
```
Return twice to DS.
```
2 a fad; a fad; as a lad; as a lad; all ads; all ads
```
DS
```
3 as a fad; as a fad; a sad lass; a sad lass; a fall
```
DS
```
4 ask a lad; ask a lad; all jaks fall; all jaks fall
```
DS
```
5 a sad fall; a sad fall; all fall ads; all fall ads
```
DS
```
6 add a jak; a lad asks a lass; as a jak ad all fall
```

RH ◆
End-of-Lesson Routine

1. Exit the software.
2. Remove from disk drive any disk you have inserted.
3. Store materials.

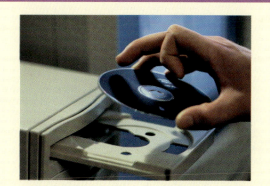
Disk removal

Most computer manufacturers recommend turning a computer off at the end of the day, rather than immediately after each use.

Enrichment

1. Key each line twice SS; DS between 2-line groups.
2. Key each line again to quicken your keystrokes if time permits.

PRACTICE CUE:
Key slowly the first time you key a line to master the required motions. As you key a line a second time, try to make each motion a bit faster.

```
1 ff jj dd kk ss ll aa ;; fj dk sl a; jf kd ls ;a a;

2 aa ;; ss ll dd kk ff jj ja js jd jf fj fk fl f; fj

3 fjf dkd sls a;a jfj kdk lsl ;a;a a;sldkfj a;sldkfj

4 fdsa jkl; asdf ;lkj all all ask ask jak jak ad add

5 a a as as ask ask ad ad lad lad add add fall falls

6 a jak ad; a sad dad; a lad asks; a lad asks a lass

7 a sad fall; all fall ads; as a lass asks a sad lad

8 as a fall fad; add a jak salad; as a sad lad falls
```

29C◆ 15
Technique Mastery

1. Key each line once at an easy, steady pace.
2. Key each line again at a quicker pace.
3. Key a 1' writing on each of lines 10, 12, and 14; find *gwam* on each writing.
4. Key 1 or 2 more 1' writings on the two slower lines.

underline & CAPS LOCK
1 <u>Ballet & Modern Dance</u>; <u>The Encyclopedia of Film</u>; <u>American Theatre</u>
2 Marilou has bought TEN OF THE BEST of the <u>Reader's Digest</u> series.

shift keys
3 The Royal Ballet; Nederlands Dans Theater; London Festival Ballet
4 Balanchine and Kirstein founded the New York City Ballet in 1948.

apostrophe & quotes
5 Masefield's "The Dauber"; Kipling's "Gunga Din"; Bronte's "Hope";
6 We'll read Sandburg's "Chicago" and Frost's "The Road Not Taken."

alphabet
7 hope very quit mark axle zone cord boat sign four gown such major
8 Six able men have quietly walked off good jobs at our city plaza.

letter response
9 date upon ever only care jump sets pink fear join were milk defer
10 As you are aware, my trade union acted upon only a few age cases.

combination response
11 fish were duty ever risk fear goal fast they safe sign hulk ivory
12 You are to refer the big wage case to an auto union panel of six.

word response
13 then form their eight world visit title chair firms signal profit
14 A city auditor is to sign all the work forms for the civic panel.

| 1 | 2 | 3 | 4 | 5 | 6 | 7 | 8 | 9 | 10 | 11 | 12 | 13 |

29D◆ 15
Skillbuilding: Straight Copy

1. Key a 1' writing on ¶ 1; find *gwam*.
2. Key two 1' *guided* writings on ¶ 1. (See p. 45 for help with guided writing procedure.)
3. Key ¶ 2 in the same manner.
4. Key two 3' writings on ¶s 1-2 together; find *gwam* and count errors on each writing.

Quarter-Minute Checkpoints

gwam	1/4'	1/2'	3/4'	Time
20	5	10	15	20
24	6	12	18	24
28	7	14	21	28
32	8	16	24	32
36	9	18	27	36
40	10	20	30	40
44	11	22	33	44
48	12	24	36	48
52	13	26	39	52
56	14	28	42	56

The **a** above these ¶s shows that they are of average difficulty.

 all letters used

3'

Words are the building blocks of effective writing.   The   4 | 44
better we put our ideas into words, the more likely we are to   8 | 48
persuade the reader to do what we ask.   If our letters ramble,   12 | 52
are not clear, or exhibit poor grammar, we increase the likeli-   16 | 56
hood of having our ideas rejected and our requests denied.   20 | 60

Any weak letter can be improved by rewriting so that the   24 | 64
final copy quickly conveys its basic ideas in a clear, exact man-   28 | 68
ner.   The reader should not then need to puzzle over its meaning.   33 | 73
All features of style and content should be designed to enhance   37 | 77
the meaning instead of to distract from it.   40 | 80

| 1 | 2 | 3 | 4 |

Lesson 2

New Keys: H and E

Objectives:

1. To learn reach technique for H and E.
2. To combine smoothly H and E with home keys.

2A◆

Get Ready to Key

At the beginning of each practice session, follow the *Standard Plan* given at the right to get ready to key the lesson.

Standard Plan for Getting Ready to Key

1. Arrange work area as shown on p. 1.
2. Check to see that the computer, monitor, and printer (if any) are plugged in.
3. Turn on the computer and monitor.
4. Open your word processing or *MicroType* program (Start menu) if it is not open. (When the program is open, you will see a button with the name of the program at the bottom of the computer screen.) Choose the Open Screen in *MicroType*.
5. Align the front of the keyboard with the front edge of the desk or table.
6. Position the monitor and this book for easy reading.

Note: If *MicroType Pro* or *MicroType Multimedia* is available (see p. xiii), use it after each lesson in Unit 2. Once you finish a lesson in this book, open the Alphabetic Keyboarding section in *MicroType* and do the corresponding lesson.

2B◆

Plan for Learning New Keys

All keys except the home keys (**FDSA JKL;**) require the fingers to reach in order to strike them. Follow the *Standard Plan* given at the right in learning the proper reach for each new key.

Standard Plan for Learning New Keys

1. Find the new key on the keyboard chart given on the page where the new key is introduced.
2. Look at your own keyboard and find the new key on it.
3. Study the reach-technique picture at the left of the practice lines for the new key. (See p. 9 for illustrations.) Read the statement below the illustration.
4. Identify the finger to be used to strike the new key.
5. Curve your fingers; place them in home-key position (over **FDSA JKL;**).
6. Watch your finger as you reach it to the new key and back to home position a few times (keep it curved).
7. Refer to the set of 3 drill lines at the right of the reach-technique illustration. Key each line twice SS (single-spaced):
   - once slowly, to learn new reach;
   - then faster, for a quick-snap stroke. DS (double-space) between 2-line groups.

2C◆

Home-Key Review

each line twice single-spaced (SS): once slowly; again, at a faster pace; double-space (DS) between 2-line groups

All keystrokes learned

```
1 a;sldkfj a; sl dk fj ff jj dd kk ss ll aa ;; fj a;

2 as as ad ad all all jak jak fad fad fall fall lass

3 a jak; a fad; as a lad; ask dad; a lass; a fall ad
```

Return 4 times to quadruple-space (QS) between lesson parts.

Lessons 29-30

Keyboard Mastery & Skill Assessment
Lesson 29 Keyboard Mastery

O b j e c t i v e s :
1. **To reinforce/improve keyboard mastery.**
2. **To improve technique/speed on straight copy.**

29A◆ 5
Conditioning Practice

1. Key each line once; then key each line again faster.
2. Key a 1' writing on line 3; find *gwam*.

alphabet	1	Five or six people jogged quickly along the beach in a warm haze.
fig/sym	2	This Chu & Son's May 17 check should be $45.39 instead of $62.80.
speed	3	Lana and he may cycle to the ancient city chapel by the big lake.

| 1 | 2 | 3 | 4 | 5 | 6 | 7 | 8 | 9 | 10 | 11 | 12 | 13 |

29B◆ 15
Keyboard Review

1. Key each line once at an easy, steady pace.
2. Key each line again at a quicker pace.
3. If time permits, rekey lines that were awkward or difficult for you.

Technique goals
- curved, upright fingers
- quick-snap keystrokes
- no finger "flyout"
- down-and-in spacing
- eyes on copy

A/Z	1	Zoe had a pizza at the plaza by the zoo on a lazy, hazy day.
B/Y	2	Abby may be too busy to buy me a book for my long boat trip.
C/X	3	Zeno caught six cod to fix lunch for his six excited scouts.
D/W	4	Wilda would like to own the wild doe she found in the woods.
E/V	5	Evan will give us the van to move the five very heavy boxes.
F/U	6	All four of us bought coats with faux fur collars and cuffs.
G/T	7	Eight guys tugged the big boat into deep water to get going.
H/S	8	Marsha wishes to show us how to make charts on the computer.
I/R	9	Ira will rise above his ire to rid the firm of this problem.
J/Q	10	Quen just quietly quit the squad after a major joint injury.
K/P	11	Kip packed a backpack and put it on an oak box on the porch.
L/O	12	Lola is to wear the royal blue skirt and a gold wool blouse.
M/N	13	Many of the men met in the main hall to see the new manager.
figures	14	I worked from 8:30 to 5 at 1964 Lake Blvd. from May 7 to 26.
fig/sym	15	I quote, "ISBN #0-651-24876-3 was assigned to them in 1999."

Lesson 29

2D◆
New Keys: H and E

Use the *Standard Plan for Learning New Keys* (p. 8) for each key to be learned. Study the plan now.

Relate each step of the plan to the illustrations below and copy at right. Then key each line twice SS; leave a DS between 2-line groups.

h *Right index* finger

e *Left middle* finger

Do not attempt to key the headings (Learn h), line numbers, or vertical lines separating word groups.

Learn h

1 j j hj hj ah ah ha ha had had has has ash ash hash
2 hj hj ha ha ah ah hah hah had had ash ash has hash
3 ah ha; had ash; has had; a hall; has a hall; ah ha
Return twice to double-space (DS) after you complete the set of lines.

Learn e

4 d d ed ed el el led led eel eel eke eke ed fed fed
5 ed ed el el lee lee fed fed eke eke led led ale ed
6 a lake; a leek; a jade; a desk; a jade eel; a deed

Combine h and e

7 he he he | she she she | shed shed | heed heed | held held
8 a lash; a shed; he held; she has jade; held a sash
9 has fled; he has ash; she had jade; she had a sale
Return 4 times to quadruple-space (QS) between lesson parts.

2E◆
New-Key Mastery

1. Key the lines once SS; DS between 2-line groups.
2. Key the lines again with quick, sharp strokes at a faster pace.

Fingers curved

Fingers upright

SPACING CUE:

Space once after ; used as punctuation.

Once the screen is filled with keyed lines, the top line disappears when a new line is added at the bottom. This is called **scrolling**.

home row
1 ask ask|has has|lad lad|all all|jak jak|fall falls
2 a jak; a lad; a sash; had all; has a jak; all fall

h/e
3 he he|she she|led led|held held|jell jell|she shed
4 he led; she had; she fell; a jade ad; a desk shelf

all keys learned
5 elf elf|all all|ask ask|led led|jak jak|hall halls
6 ask dad; he has jell; she has jade; he sells leeks

all keys learned
7 he led; she has; a jak ad; a jade eel; a sled fell
8 she asked a lad; he led all fall; she has all jade

28E◆   16

New Keys: = and [ ]

1. Locate the appropriate symbol on the keyboard chart.
2. Key each line twice SS; DS between 2-line pairs.
3. If time permits, rekey lines 5-7.

TECHNIQUE CUE:

=   Strike = with the right little finger.

[ ]   Strike either [or] with the right little finger.

Two uses of brackets are
- To enclose explanations in quoted copy.
- To show—along with parentheses—units within larger units in mathematical formulas. Brackets are not used in place of parentheses.

= = "equal" sign
[ ] = brackets

Learn =

1   = =; = =; = = =; = = = =; ='='='='='='; if 3x = 15, then x = 5
2   Change your answer to 12x = 16; if 8x = 24, does x = 2 or 3?

Learn [ ]

3   [;[;   ]']'   ['['   ]']'   ]'[']'   [sic]   [loco]   (we [Al and I] left)
4   "They [those arriving last] knew this [the pin] was stolen."

Combine = and [ ]

5   "If 2 + 2 = 2," she [Ana] said, "we are in serious trouble."
6   Work a problem: z = [2(x + y)] + [4(x + 6y)]; x = 3; y = 5.
7   If x = 11 and y = 5, what does 9[(8x + 2y - 4x) + 2y] equal?

| 1 | 2 | 3 | 4 | 5 | 6 | 7 | 8 | 9 | 10 | 11 | 12 |

28F◆   14

New Keys: > and <

1. Locate the appropriate symbol on the keyboard chart.
2. Key each line twice SS; DS between 2-line pairs.
3. If time permits, rekey lines 5-7.

TECHNIQUE CUE:

>   Depress the left shift key; strike > with the right ring finger.

<   Depress the left shift key; strike < with the right middle finger.

The > and < often appear in Web site addresses and lines of computer code. In expressions of mathematical value, the symbols stand for "greater than" and "lesser than."

> = "greater than" sign
< = "less than" sign

Learn >

1   >. >. >>.> >>.>; 19 > 23; 161 > 150; 576 > 245; 2022 > 2020.
2   If a < b, then a + c < b + c and c + a < c + b; and ac < bc.

Learn <

3   <, <, <<,< <<,<; 18 < 19; 222 < 229; 402 < 433; 5003 < 5010.
4   These are mathematical sentences: 5 + 1 < 8; a < 9; 2b < c.

Combine > and <

5   Please solve these problems: x + 8 > 9; 1 < y < 6; 5x > 10.
6   X's objectives > Y's but < C's. A's scores > B's but < D's.
7   If 2a > 3b and 3b > 4y, is y > or < a? Can you prove x > y?

| 1 | 2 | 3 | 4 | 5 | 6 | 7 | 8 | 9 | 10 | 11 | 12 |

Lesson 28

Lesson 3

New Keys: I and R

3A◆   3

Get Ready to Key

Follow the steps on p. 8.

3B◆   5

Conditioning Practice

each line twice SS; DS between 2-line groups

Practice goals
- Key each line first at a slow, steady pace, striking and releasing each key quickly.
- Key each line again at a faster pace; move from key to key quickly–keep insertion point moving steadily.

home keys 1   a;sldkfj a;sldkfj as jak ask fad all dad lads fall
Return twice to DS.

h/e 2   hj hah has had sash hash ed led fed fled sled fell
DS

all keys learned 3   as he fled; ask a lass; she had jade; sell all jak
Return 4 times to quadruple-space (QS) between lesson parts.

3C◆   5

Speed Building

each line once DS

SPACING CUE:

To DS when in SS mode, strike **Return/Enter** twice at the end of each line.

SPEED CUE:

In lines 1-3, quicken the keying pace as you key each letter combination or word when it is repeated within the line.

1   hj hj|ah ah|ha ha|had had|ash ash|has has|had hash

2   ed ed|el el|ed ed|led led|eke eke|lee lee|ale kale

3   he he|she she|led led|has has|held held|sled sleds

4   he fled; she led; she had jade; he had a jell sale

5   a jak fell; she held a leek; he has had a sad fall

6   he has ash; she sells jade; as he fell; has a lake

7   she had a fall jade sale; he leads all fall sales;

8   he held a fall kale sale; she sells leeks as a fad

Lesson 3

28C◆   14
New Keys: ! and \

1. Locate the appropriate symbol on the keyboard chart.
2. Key each line twice; DS between 2-line pairs.
3. If time permits, rekey lines 5-7.

The backslash (\) is used as a separator in computer filenames and in programming language. It should not be used in place of the diagonal (/).

The location of the backslash may vary from one keyboard to another.

TECHNIQUE CUE:
! Depress the right shift key; strike ! with the left little finger.
\ Reach up or down to strike \ with the right little finger (depending on its location on your keyboard).

! = Exclamation point
\ = Backslash

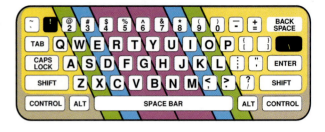

Learn !
1 !a !a!qa Ha! No! Watch out! Get set! Get ready! Go now!
2 Too bad! Not now! Listen to the siren! I won the contest!

Learn \
3 \; \; \;' \;'; '\' '\'; \\\'\ \\\'\; cd\c; cd\b; cd\d; b*.*
4 Change to d:\window\psfonts to copy fonts to e:\psfonts\new.

Combine ! and \
5 Don't erase c:\arts.doc! Save it to e:\docs before closing!
6 Back up c:\fonts now! The directory, c:\fonts, has changed!
7 Rush e:\gam\5.eps and f:\pho\9.eps to johnarns@caps.net now!

| 1 | 2 | 3 | 4 | 5 | 6 | 7 | 8 | 9 | 10 | 11 | 12 |

28D◆   14
Build Skill

1. Key three 1' writings; find *gwam*.
2. Key two 2' writings; find *gwam*.
3. Compare *gwam* rates.

	1'	2'
As strange as it may seem, you are never too young to	12	6
start thinking about retirement. Certainly, the younger you	24	12
are when you begin to contemplate about your older years,	36	18
the easier it will be to retire. Do you want to retire when	48	24
you are young enough to enjoy it? To be able to do just that,	60	30
you will have to begin preparing early. Following some obvious	73	37
rules can help. Always pay yourself first. Calculate a reason-	86	43
able amount of money that you can put into savings each month	98	49
and pay this amount zealously. Purchase permanent life insur-	110	55
ance early so that the rates will be less, and the policy will	123	62
be paid up early. Spend a large quantity of your paycheck	135	67
on items that will accrue in value: An expensive car, for	147	73
instance, is a bad investment; a house is much better.	158	79

| 1 | 2 | 3 | 4 | 5 | 6 | 7 | 8 | 9 | 10 | 11 | 12 |
| 1 | | 2 | | 3 | | 4 | | 5 | | 6 | |

3D◆ 18
New Keys: I and R

each line twice SS (slowly, then faster); DS between 2-line groups; if time permits, key lines 7-9 again

Technique goals
- curved, upright fingers
- finger-action keystrokes
- eyes on copy

i *Right middle* finger

r *Left index* finger

Follow the *Standard Plan for Learning New Keys* outlined on p. 8.

Learn i

1 k k ik ik is is if if did did aid aid kid kid hail
2 ik ik if if is is kid kid his his lie lie aid aide
3 a kid; a lie; if he; he did; his aide; if a kid is
                                                    DS

Learn r

4 f f rf rf jar jar her her are are ark ark jar jars
5 rf rf re re fr fr jar jar red red her her far fare
6 a jar; a rake; a lark; red jar; hear her; are dark
                                                    DS

Combine i and r

7 fir fir|rid rid|sir sir|ire ire|fire fire|air airs
8 a fir; if her; a fire; is fair; his ire; if she is
9 he is; if her; is far; red jar; his heir; her aide
                            Quadruple-space (QS) between lesson parts.

3E◆ 19
New-Key Mastery

1. Key the lines once SS with a DS between 2-line groups.
2. Key the lines again at a faster pace.

Technique goals
- fingers deeply curved
- wrists low, but not resting
- hands/arms steady
- eyes on copy as you key

reach review
1 hj ed ik rf hj de ik fr hj ed ik rf jh de ki fr hj
2 he he|if if|all all|fir fir|jar jar|rid rid|as ask
                                                    DS

h/e
3 she she|elf elf|her her|hah hah|eel eel|shed shelf
4 he has; had jak; her jar; had a shed; she has fled
                                                    DS

i/r
5 fir fir|rid rid|sir sir|kid kid|ire ire|fire fired
6 a fir; is rid; is red; his ire; her kid; has a fir
                                                    DS

all keys learned
7 if if|is is|he he|did did|fir fir|jak jak|all fall
8 a jak; he did; ask her; red jar; she fell; he fled
                                                    DS

all keys learned
9 if she is; he did ask; he led her; he has her jar;
10 she has had a jak sale; she said he had a red fir;

Lesson 3

Lesson 28

New Keys: @, +, !, \, =, [ ], >, and <

Objectives:
1. To learn reach-strokes for @, +, !, \, =, [ ], >, and <.
2. To combine smoothly @, +, !, \, =, [ ], >, and < with other keys.

28A◆ 5

Conditioning Practice

each line twice SS; then a 1' writing on line 3; find *gwam*

alphabet 1 Zak never exactly said the lamps were being made for Jacque.

figures 2 I bought 248 zip disks, 50 drives, and 63 modems on 7/14/98.

easy 3 Sidney lent the auto to us to aid the girl in the ruby gown.

| 1 | 2 | 3 | 4 | 5 | 6 | 7 | 8 | 9 | 10 | 11 | 12 |

28B◆ 14

New Keys: @ and +

1. Locate the appropriate symbol on the keyboard chart.
2. Key each line twice SS; DS between 2-line pairs.
3. If time permits, rekey lines 5-7.

The @ is a common character in e-mail addresses and in prices of items for sale.

TECHNIQUE CUE:

@ Depress the right shift key; strike @ with the left ring finger.
+ Depress the left shift key; strike + with the right little finger.

@ = "at" sign
+ = "plus" sign

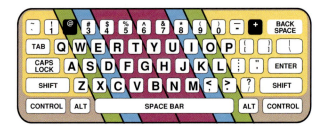

Learn @

1 s s s@ s@ s@ @sw @sxw @sxw; 32 @ .45; 65 @ .99; sold 2 @ .10
2 Buy 44 @ .98; sell 64 @ .52; hold 337 @ .19; ship 120 @ .22.

Learn +

3 + ;+ ;+ +;+ +;+; 5 + 5 or 4 + 4; A+, B+, or C+; 9 + 9; 2 + 2
4 Kim got an A+ after adding 99 + 106 + 100 + 97 + 103 points.

Combine @ and +

5 E-mail Ty at lbeckett@waco.com; Lilly at lilbertz@capso.net.
6 Buy 5 bonds @ 22.91 + 3 stocks @ 32.11 + 10 T-bills @ 45.31.
7 Add Order Nos. 6 + 9 + 81; send an invoice to cruis@mgt.com.

| 1 | 2 | 3 | 4 | 5 | 6 | 7 | 8 | 9 | 10 | 11 | 12 |

Review

O b j e c t i v e s :
1. **To improve reach-stroke control and keying speed.**
2. **To improve technique on Space Bar and Enter.**

RA◆ 3
Get Ready to Key

1. Review the steps for arranging your work area (see p. 1).
2. Review the steps required to ready your equipment.
3. Take good keying position.

- fingers curved and upright
- wrists low, but not touching frame of keyboard
- forearms parallel to slant of keyboard
- body erect, sitting back in chair
- feet on floor for balance

RB◆ 5
Conditioning Practice

each line twice SS; DS between 2-line groups

1 a;sldkfj fj dk sl a; jh de ki fr hj ed ik rf fj a;

2 a if is el he la as re led fir did she has jak jar

3 he has fir; she had a jak; a jade jar; a leek sale

QS

RC◆ 10
Technique: Space Bar

1. Key lines 1-6 once SS; DS between 3-line groups. Space *immediately* after each word.
2. Key the lines again at a faster pace.

Use down-and-in motion

Short, easy words

1 if is ha la ah el as re id did sir fir die rid lie

2 as lad lei rah jak had ask lid her led his kid has

3 hah all ire add iris hall fire keel sell jeer fall

DS

Short-word phrases

4 if he|he is|if he is|if she|she is|if she is|as is

5 as he is|if he led|if she has|if she did|had a jak

6 as if|a jar lid|all her ads|as he said|a jade fish

QS

RD◆ 10
Technique: Return

each line twice SS; DS between 2-line groups

1 if he is;
2 as if she is;
3 he had a fir desk;
4 she has a red jell jar;
5 he has had a lead all fall;
6 she asked if he reads fall ads;
7 she said she reads all ads she sees;
8 his dad has had a sales lead as he said;

QS

Reach out and tap Return/Enter.

PRACTICE CUE:
Keep up your pace to the end of the line, return quickly, and begin the new line without a pause or stop.

27C◆ 16
New Keys: _ and *

1. Locate new symbol on appropriate keyboard chart.
2. Key twice SS the appropriate pair of lines given at right; DS between pairs.
3. Repeat Steps 1 and 2 for the other new key.
4. Key twice SS lines 5-8.

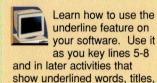 Learn how to use the underline feature on your software. Use it as you key lines 5-8 and in later activities that show underlined words, titles, etc.

Underline: Depress left shift; strike _ (shift of –) with right little finger.

Asterisk: Depress left shift; strike * (shift of 8) with right middle finger.

Learn _ (underline)

1 ; ; _; _; ;; __ ;_; ;_; I _____ go there; she _____ go also.
2 They ___ to visit _____ aunt, but _____ cousin __ at school.

Learn * (asterisk)

3 k k *k *k kk ** k*k k*k She used * for a single source note.
4 All discounted items show an *, thus: 48K*, 588*, and 618*.

Combine _ and *

5 Use an * to mark often-confused words such as <u>then</u> and <u>than</u>.
6 *Note: Book titles (like <u>Lorna Doone</u>) are often underlined.
7 I saw a review of "La Casa Verde" in <u>Latin American Fiction</u>.
8 Did you view <u>Hornblower</u>--a 12th century African sculpture?

27D◆ 13
Statistical Copy

1. Key two 1' and two 2' writings on the ¶; find *gwam* on each.
2. Key a 3' writing on the ¶; find *gwam*.

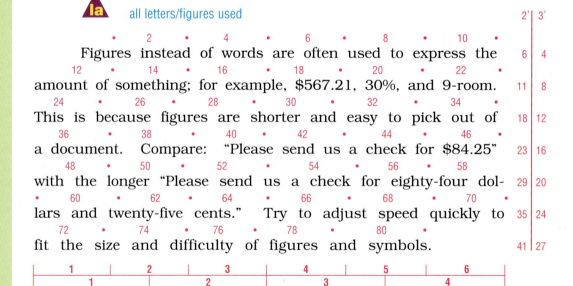

la   all letters/figures used

	2'	3'
Figures instead of words are often used to express the	6	4
amount of something; for example, $567.21, 30%, and 9-room.	11	8
This is because figures are shorter and easy to pick out of	18	12
a document. Compare: "Please send us a check for $84.25"	23	16
with the longer "Please send us a check for eighty-four dol-	29	20
lars and twenty-five cents." Try to adjust speed quickly to	35	24
fit the size and difficulty of figures and symbols.	41	27

RE◆ 10
Speed Building: Words

1. Key each line once SS; DS below line 3.
2. Key each line again at a faster pace; QS (4 hard returns) at end of drill.

PRACTICE CUE:

Key the first word of each pair at an easy speed: rekey it at a faster speed. *Think* and *say* each word; key it with quick-snap strokes.

Fingers curved

Goal: to speed up the combining of letters

1 is is|if if|ah ah|he he|el el|irk irk|aid aid|aide
2 as as|ask ask|ad ad|had had|re re|ire ire|are hare
3 if if|fir fir|id id|did did|el el|eel eel|jak jaks

QS

RF◆ 12
Speed Building: Phrases

1. Key each line once SS.
2. Key the lines once more to improve your speed.

PRACTICE CUE:

Speed up the second keying of each phrase: Space quickly between words and phrases.

Space with right thumb

Use down-and-in motion

Goal: to speed up spacing between words

1 ah ha|ah ha|if he|if he|as if|as if|as he|as he is
2 if a|if a|a fir|a fir|a jar|a jar|irk her|irks her
3 he did|he did|if all|if all|if she led|if she fled
4 a lad|a lad|if her|if her|as his aide|as his aides

Enrichment

1. Key the drill once SS at an easy pace to gain control of all your reach-stroke motions. DS between 2-line groups.
2. Key the drill again to speed up your motions and build continuity (keeping the insertion point moving steadily across the screen).

reach review
1 hj ed ik rf jh de ki fr jhj ded kik frf hj ed ik ;
2 he if fir sir she jar rid ask led kid his did risk

h/e
3 he el she elf her led had held desk dash jade fled
4 her dad led; a lad fled; he has jade; she had eel;

i/r
5 is his kid ski fir rid ire die slid kids fife dike
6 a kid led; she is fair; as her aide; he is a risk;

all keys learned
7 if a jail; as he fled; risk a lead; has a red sled
8 a jade fish; ask if she slid; she has irked a kid;

all keys learned
9 as if he did; he asked a lad; his dad has red jars
10 he has a sled; if she has a jar; ask if he is here

L e s s o n   2 7

New Keys: ', ", _, and *

O b j e c t i v e s :

1. To learn reach-strokes for ', ", _, and *.
2. To combine ', ", _, and * smoothly with other keys.

27A◆ 5
Conditioning Practice

each line twice SS; then a 1'
writing on line 3; find *gwam*

alphabet 1 Bowman fixed prized clocks that seven judges say are unique.
figures 2 Only 1,453 of the 6,270 members were at the 1998 convention.
easy 3 She lent the field auditor a hand with the work of the firm.

| 1 | 2 | 3 | 4 | 5 | 6 | 7 | 8 | 9 | 10 | 11 | 12 |

27B◆ 16
New Keys: ' and "

1. Locate new symbol on appropriate keyboard chart; read technique statement below the chart.
2. Key twice SS the appropriate pair of lines given at right; DS between pairs.
3. Repeat Steps 1 and 2 for the other new symbol.
4. Key twice SS lines 5-8.
5. Rekey the lines with which you had difficulty.

> ### CAPITALIZATION CUE:
> Capitalize first word and all other important words in titles of publications.

Apostrophe: ' is to the right of ; and is controlled by the right little finger.

Quotation mark: Depress left shift and strike " (shift of ') with the right little finger.

> The quotation marks that you key will look the same whether at the beginning or end of a quotation. Notice in the copy below, however, that the opening and closing marks are not the same.

Learn ' (apostrophe)

1 ; ; '; '; ;; " ;'; ;'; it's he's I'm I've It's hers, I see.
2 I'm not sure if it's Hal's; but if it's his, I'll return it.

Learn " (quotation mark)

3 ; ; "; "; ;; "" ;"; ;"; "Keep on," she said, but I had quit.
4 I read "Ode on a Grecian Urn," "The Last Leaf," and "Trees."

Combine ' and "

5 "If it's Jan's or Al's," she said, "I'll bring it to class."
6 "Its" is an adjective; "it's" is the contraction of ' "it is."
7 Miss Uhl said, "To make numbers plural, add 's: 8's, 10's."
8 O'Shea said, "Use ' (apostrophe) to shorten phrases: I'll."

Lesson 4

New Keys: O and T

Objectives:

1. To learn reach technique for O and T.
2. To combine smoothly O and T with all other learned keys.

4A ◆ 8

Conditioning Practice

each line twice SS (slowly, then faster); DS between 2-line groups

In Lessons 4-8, the time for the *Conditioning Practice* is changed to 8'. During this time, you are to arrange your work area, prepare your equipment for keying, and practice the lines of the *Conditioning Practice* as directed.

Fingers curved

Fingers upright

home row 1 a sad fall; ask a lass; a jak falls; as a fall ad;

3d row 2 if her aid; all he sees; he irks her; a jade fish;

all keys learned 3 as he fell; he sells fir desks; she had half a jar

---

4B ◆ 20

New Keys: O and T

each line twice SS (slowly, then faster); DS between 2-line groups; if time permits, key lines 7-9 again

o *Right ring* finger

t *Left index* finger

Follow the *Standard Plan for Learning New Keys* outlined on p. 8.

Learn o

1 l l ol ol do do of of so so lo lo old old for fore

2 ol ol of of or or for for oak oak off off sol sole

3 do so; a doe; of old; of oak; old foe; of old oak;
DS

Learn t

4 f f tf tf it it at at tie tie the the fit fit lift

5 tf tf ft ft it it sit sit fit fit hit hit kit kite

6 if it; a fit; it fit; tie it; the fit; at the site
DS

Combine o and t

7 to to|too too|toe toe|dot dot|lot lot|hot hot|tort

8 a lot; to jot; too hot; odd lot; a fort; for a lot

9 of the; to rot; dot it; the lot; for the; for this
QS

Lesson 4

26C♦ 16
New Keys: (and)

each set of lines twice SS (slowly, then faster); DS between groups; if time permits, practice the lines again

TECHNIQUE CUE:

(Depress the left shift key; then strike (with right ring finger.

) Depress the left shift key; then strike) with right little finger.

SPACING CUE:

Do not space between ( ) and copy they enclose.

(= left parenthesis
) = right parenthesis

Learn (

use the letter "l"

1 l l (l (l ll ((l(l l(l 9(9(Shift for the (as you key (9.
2 As (is the shift of 9, use the l finger to key 9, (, or (9.

Learn)

3 ; ;);); ;:)) ;); ;); 0) 0) Shift for the) as you key 0).
4 As) is the shift of 0, use the ; finger to key 0,), or 0).

Combine (and)

5 Hints: (1) depress shift; (2) strike key; (3) release both.
6 Tab steps: (1) clear tabs, (2) set stops, and (3) tabulate.
7 The new account (#594-7308) draws annual interest at 3 1/4%.

26D♦ 7
Skillbuilding

1. Key lines 1-8 once SS.
2. Key a 1' writing on line 7 and then on line 8; find *gwam* on each sentence.
3. Key a 1' and a 2' writing on the ¶; find *gwam* on each writing.

& and #

1 Rios & Cho will try Case #947-285 and Case #960-318 in June.
2 DP&L sent Invoice #67-5849-302 to Ito & Brown on October 19.

(and)

3 Waltz (the plaintiff) and Ross (the defendant) are in court.
4 The note for five hundred dollars ($500) pays 8.5% interest.

basic symbols

5 Twenty-four (31%) of the owners voted for a $250 assessment.
6 Only 1/4 picked Yes, 1/2 picked No, and 1/4 did not respond.

easy sentences

7 Did the girl row to the dock for the clams and six big fish?
8 They wish to make an issue of the work she did for the city.

| 1 | 2 | 3 | 4 | 5 | 6 | 7 | 8 | 9 | 10 | 11 | 12 |

26E♦ 6
Skill Check

Key a 1' and a 2' writing on the ¶; find *gwam* on each writing.

la all letters used

2'

• 2 • 4 • 6 • 8 • 10 •

When you key copy that contains both words and numbers,   6

12 • 14 • 16 • 18 • 20 • 22 •

it is best to key numbers using the top row. When the copy   12

24 • 26 • 28 • 30 • 32 • 34 •

consists primarily of figures, however, it may be faster to   18

36 • 38 • 40 • 42 • 44 • 46 •

use the keypad. In any event, keying figures quickly is a   24

48 • 50 • 52 • 54 • 56 • 58

major skill to prize. You can expect to key figures often   30

• 60 • 62 • 64 • 66 • 68 • 70 •

in the future, so learn to key them with very little peeking.   36

| 1 | 2 | 3 | 4 | 5 | 6 |

4C ◆ 22
New-Key Mastery

1. Key the lines once SS; DS between 2-line groups.
2. Key the lines again at a faster pace.

Technique goals
- curved, upright fingers
- wrists low, but not resting
- down-and-in spacing
- eyes on copy as you key

PRACTICE CUE:

In lines of repeated words (lines 3, 5, and 7), speed up the second keying of each word.

reach review
1 hj ed ik rf ol tf jh de ki fr lo ft hj ed ol rf tf
2 is led fro hit old fit let kit rod kid dot jak sit

h/e
3 he he|she she|led led|had had|see see|has has|seek
4 he led|ask her|she held|has fled|had jade|he leads

i/t
5 it it|fit fit|tie tie|sit sit|kit kit|its its|fits
6 a kit|a fit|a tie|lit it|it fits|it sits|it is fit

o/r
7 or or|for for|ore ore|fro fro|oar oar|roe roe|rode
8 a rod|a door|a rose|or for|her or|he rode|or a rod

space bar
9 of he or it is to if do el odd off too for she the
10 it is|if it|do so|if he|to do|or the|she is|of all

all keys learned
11 if she is; ask a lad; to the lake; for the old jet
12 he or she; for a fit; if she left the; a jak salad

Enrichment

1. Key the drill once SS at an easy pace to gain control of all your reach-stroke motions. DS between 2-line groups.
2. Key the drill again to speed up your motions and build continuity (keeping the insertion point moving steadily across the screen).

reach review
1 hj ed ik rf jhj ded kik frf a;sldkfj a;sldkfj fja;
2 if led ski fir she ire sir jak has did jar kid rid

o/t
3 ol ol|old old|for for|oak oak|ode ode|doe doe|does
4 tf tf|it it|to to|kit kit|the the|fit fit|sit sits

i/r
5 ik ik|if if|it it|fir fir|ski ski|did did|kid kids
6 rf rf|or or|for for|her her|fir fir|rod rod|or for

h/e
7 hj hj|he he|ah ah|ha ha|he he|she she|ash ash|hash
8 ed ed|el el|he he|her her|elk elk|jet jet|she|shed

all keys learned
9 of hot kit old sit for jet she oak jar ore lid lot
10 a ski; old oak; too hot; odd jar; for the; old jet

all keys learned
11 she is to ski; is for the lad; ask if she has jade
12 he sold skis for her; she sells jade at their lake

Lesson 4

LEARN O AND T

15

Lesson 26

New Keys: #, &, (, and)

Objectives:

1. To learn reach-strokes for #, &, (, and).
2. To combine #, &, (, and) smoothly with other keys.

26A◆ 5

Conditioning Practice

each line twice SS; then a 1'
writing on line 3; find *gwam*

alphabet 1 Racquel just put back five azure gems next to my gold watch.

figures 2 Joel used a comma in 1,203 and 2,946 but not in 583 and 750.

easy 3 The auto firm owns the big signs by the downtown civic hall.

| 1 | 2 | 3 | 4 | 5 | 6 ↓ 7 | 8 | 9 | 10 | 11 | 12 |

26B◆ 16

New Keys: # and &

each set of lines twice SS (slowly,
then faster); DS between groups;
if time permits, practice the lines
again

TECHNIQUE CUE:

\# Depress the right shift
key; then strike # with
left middle finger.

& Depress the left shift
key; then strike & with
right index finger.

= number/pounds
& = ampersand (and)

Do not space between #
and a figure; space once
before and after & used
to join names.

Learn # (number/pounds)

1 d d #d #d dd ## d#d d#d 3# 3# Shift for # as you enter #33d.
2 Do not space between a number and #: 3# of #633 at $9.35/#.

Learn & (ampersand)

3 j j &j &j jj && j&j j&j 7& 7& Have you written to Poe & Son?
4 Do not space before or after & in initials, e.g., CG&E, B&O.

Combine # and &

5 Shift for # and &. Recall: # stands for number and pounds.
6 Names joined by & require spaces; a # sign alone does, also.
7 Letters joined by & are keyed solid: List Stock #3 as C&NW.
8 I bought 20# of #830 grass seed from Locke & Uhl on March 4.

Lesson 5

New Keys: N and G

Objectives:

1. To learn reach technique for N and G.
2. To combine smoothly N and G with all other learned keys.

5A◆ 8

Conditioning Practice

each line twice SS (slowly, then faster); DS between 2-line groups

home row 1 has a jak; ask a lad; a fall fad; had a jak salad;

o/t 2 to do it; as a tot; do a lot; it is hot; to dot it

e/i/r 3 is a kid; it is far; a red jar; her skis; her aide

5B◆ 20

New Keys: N and G

each line twice SS (slowly, then faster); DS between 2-line groups; if time permits, key lines 7-9 again

n *Right index* finger

g *Left index* finger

Follow the *Standard Plan for Learning New Keys* outlined on p. 8.

Learn n

1 j j nj nj an an and and end end ant ant land lands

2 nj nj an an en en in in on on end end and and hand

3 an en; an end; an ant; no end; on land; a fine end

Learn g

4 f f gf gf go go fog fog got got fig figs jogs jogs

5 gf gf go go got got dig dig jog jog logs logs golf

6 to go; he got; to jog; to jig; the fog; is to golf

Combine n and g

7 go go|no no|nag nag|ago ago|gin gin|gone gone|long

8 go on; a nag; sign in; no gain; long ago; into fog

9 a fine gig; log in soon; a good sign; lend a hand;

5C◆ 5

Technique: Return

each line twice SS; DS between 2-line groups

PRACTICE CUE:

Keep up your pace to end of line; return quickly and start new line without pause.

Reach out and tap Return/Enter.

1 she is gone;

2 she got an old dog;

3 she jogs in a dense fog;

4 she and he go to golf at nine;

5 he is a hand on a rig in the north;

25C◆ 16
New Keys: % and - (hyphen)

each line twice SS (slowly, then faster); DS between 4-line groups; if time permits, practice the lines again

TECHNIQUE CUE:

% Depress the right shift key; then strike **%** with left index finger.

− Reach up to strike **−** with right little finger.

Some word processing software changes -- to a single character.

% = percent sign
− = hyphen
Do not space between a figure and the %, nor before or after − or − − (dash) used as punctuation.

Learn % (percent sign)

1 f f %f %f ff %% f%f f%f 5% 5% Shift for the % in 5% and 15%.
2 Do not space between a number and %:   5%, 75%, 85%, and 95%.

Learn - (hyphen)

3 ; ; -; -; ;; -- ;-; ;-; 4-ply I use a 2-ply tire on my bike.
4 I gave each film a 1-star, 2-star, 3-star, or 4-star rating.

Combine % and -

5 A dash is two unspaced hyphens--no space before or after it.
6 Kyle, send the parcel by fourth-class mail--a saving of 50%.
7 The prime rate may reach 9%--but he has no interest in that.
8 You need 40 signatures--51% of the members--on the petition.

25D◆ 7
Skillbuilding

1. Key lines 1-8 once SS.
2. Key a 1' writing on line 7 and then on line 8; find *gwam* on each sentence.

/ and $
1 Key a series of fractions as figures: 1/4, 1/3, and 1 3/10.
2 The jacket was discounted from $172.99 to $128.99 to $98.99.

% and -
3 This outlet store gives discounts of 20%, 25%, 35%, and 50%.
4 We have 1-, 2-, and 3-bath condos--he wants a separate home.

all symbols learned
5 This 10 1/2% mortgage was rewritten at 8%--a $13,496 saving.
6 These 3-part forms--minus a 10% discount--cost $75/thousand.

easy sentences
7 Shana is to key all the forms for the city auditor by eight.
8 Six of the girls do work for, me; eight do work for the city.

| 1 | 2 | 3 | 4 | 5 | 6 | 7 | 8 | 9 | 10 | 11 | 12 |

25E◆ 6
Skill Check

Key a 1' and a 2' writing on the ¶; find *gwam* on each writing.

  all letters used

	1'	2'
Just a few years ago, having the ability to operate a com-	11	6
puter was a bonus when looking for a job. Today, however, it	24	12
is an ability that is required for almost every job. Further,	36	18
you may need to key at a rapid rate and to learn the relevant	49	24
programs on the market--especially those that are needed for	61	31
your exact profession. If you can do these things, you will	73	37
be amazed at your career progress once you get the job.	84	42

| 1 | 2 | 3 | 4 | 5 | 6 | 7 | 8 | 9 | 10 | 11 | 12 |
| 1 | | 2 | | 3 | | 4 | | 5 | | 6 | |

5D ◆ 17
New-Key Mastery

1. Key the lines once SS; DS between 2-line groups.
2. Key the lines again at a faster pace.

Technique goals
- curved, upright fingers
- wrists low, but not resting
- quick-snap keystrokes
- down-and-in spacing
- eyes on copy as you key

reach review
1 a;sldkfj ed ol rf hj tf nj gf lo de jh ft nj fr a;
2 he jogs; an old ski; do a log for; she left a jar;

n/g
3 an an|go go|in in|dig dig|and and|got got|end ends
4 go to; is an; log on; sign it; and golf; fine figs

space bar
5 if if|an an|go go|of of|or or|he he|it it|is is|do
6 if it is|is to go|he or she|to do this|of the sign

all keys learned
7 she had an old oak desk; a jell jar is at the side
8 he has left for the lake; she goes there at eight;

all keys learned
9 she said he did it for her; he is to take the oars
10 sign the list on the desk; go right to the old jet

Enrichment

each line twice SS; DS between 2-line groups; QS after each grouping

Lines 1-3
curved, upright fingers; steady, easy pace

Lines 4-7
space immediately after each word; down-and-in motion of thumb

Lines 8-12
maintain pace to end of line; return quickly and start new line immediately

Lines 13-16
speed up the second keying of each repeated word or phrase; think words

Reach review
1 nj nj gf gf ol ol tf tf ik ik rf rf hj hj ed ed fj
2 go fog an and got end jog ant dog ken fig fin find
3 go an on and lag jog flag land glad lend sign hand

Spacing
4 if an it go is of do or to as in so no off too gin
5 ah ha he or if an too for and she jog got hen then
6 he is to go|if it is so|is to do it|if he is to go
7 she is to ski on the lake; he is also at the lake;

Returning
8 he is to go;
9 she is at an inn;
10 he goes to ski at one;
11 he is also to sign the log;
12 she left the log on the old desk

Keying short words and phrases
13 do do|it it|an an|is is|of of|to to|if if|or or or
14 he he|go go|in in|so so|at at|no no|as as|ha ha ha
15 to do|to do|it is|it is|of it|of it|is to|is to do
16 she is to do so; he did the sign; ski at the lake;

Lessons 25-28

Learn Symbols

Lesson 25 New Keys: /, $, %, and -

Objectives:
1. To learn reach-strokes for /, $, %, and -.
2. To combine /, $, %, and - smoothly with other keys.

25A◆ 5
Conditioning Practice

each line twice SS; then a 1'
writing on line 3; find *gwam*

alphabet 1 Di will buy from me as prizes the six unique diving jackets.

figures 2 The January 17 quiz of 25 points will test pages 389 to 460.

easy 3 Both of us may do the audit of the work of a big title firm.

| 1 | 2 | 3 | 4 | 5 | 6 | 7 | 8 | 9 | 10 | 11 | 12 |

25B◆ 16
New Keys: / and $

each line twice SS (slowly, then
faster); DS between
4-line groups; if time permits,
practice the lines again

> **TECHNIQUE CUE:**
>
> **/** Reach down to strike **/** with right little finger.
>
> **$** Depress the right shift key; strike **$** with left index finger.

> / = diagonal
> $ = dollar sign
> Do not space between a figure and the / or the $ sign.

Learn / (diagonal)

1 ; ; /; /; ;; // ;/; ;/; 2/3 4/5 and/or We keyed 1/2 and 3/4.

2 Space between a whole number and a fraction: 7 2/3, 18 3/4.

Learn $ (dollar sign)

3 f f $f $f ff $$ f$f f$f $4 $4 for $4 Shift for $ and key $4.

4 A period separates dollars and cents: $4.50, $6.25, $19.50.

Combine / and $

5 I must shift for $ but not for /: Order 10 gal. at $16/gal.

6 Do not space on either side of /: 1/6, 3/10, 9 5/8, 4 7/12.

7 We sent 5 boxes of No. 6 3/4 envelopes at $11/box on June 2.

8 They can get 2 sets of disks at $49.85/set; 10 sets, $39.85.

Lesson 25

New Keys: Left Shift and Period (.)

O b j e c t i v e s :

1. To learn reach technique for Left Shift and . (period).
2. To combine smoothly Left Shift and . (period) with all other learned keys.

Finger-action keystrokes

Down-and-in spacing

Quick out-and-tap return

6A◆   8
Conditioning Practice

each line twice SS (slowly, then faster); DS between 2-line groups

reach review	1 ed ik rf ol gf hj tf nj de ki fr lo fg jh ft jn a;
space bar	2 or is to if an of el so it go id he do as in at on
all keys learned	3 he is; if an; or do; to go; a jak; an oak; of all;

6B◆   20
New Keys: Left Shift and . (Period)

each line twice SS (slowly, then faster); DS between 2-line groups; if time permits, rekey lines 7-9

Left Shift *Left little* finger

. (period) *Right ring* finger

SHIFTING CUE:
Shift, strike key, and release both in a quick 1-2-3 count.

SPACING CUE:
Space once after . following abbreviations and initials. Do not space after . within abbreviations. Space twice after . at end of a sentence except at line endings. There, return without spacing.

Learn Left Shift key

1 a a Ja Ja Ka Ka La La Hal Hal Kal Kal Jae Jae Lana

2 Kal rode; Kae did it; Hans has jade; Jan ate a fig

3 I see that Jake is to aid Ki at the Oak Lake sale.

Learn . (period)

4 l l .l .l fl. fl. ed. ed. ft. ft. rd. rd. hr. hrs.

5 .l .l fl. fl. hr. hr. e.g. e.g. i.e. i.e. in. ins.

6 fl. ft. hr. ed. rd. rt. off. fed. ord. alt. asstd.

Combine Left Shift and . (period)

7 I do. Ian is. Ola did. Jan does. Kent is gone.

8 Hal did it. I shall do it. Kate left on a train.

9 J. L. Han skis on Oak Lake; Lt. Haig also does so.

Check Speed:
Guided Writing

1. Key a 1' writing on each ¶; find *gwam*.
2. Key a 2' and a 3' writing on ¶s 1-2 combined; find *gwam*.
3. As time permits, key 1' *guided* writings (p. 45) on each ¶ to build keying speed.

gwam	1/4'	1/2'	3/4'	Time
Quarter-Minute Checkpoints				
16	4	8	12	16
20	5	10	15	20
24	6	12	18	24
28	7	14	21	28
32	8	16	24	32
36	9	18	27	36
40	10	20	30	40

la all letters used   2' 3'

A vital difference exists between a job done right and   6   4
one done just about right.   One is given approval while the   12   8
other is not.   To receive full approval of the jobs you do,   18 12
recognize that just about right is not adequate.   Attempt   23 16
now to do every task just right.   27 18

Before long you will try problems in which are applied   32 21
the seemingly little things that are crucial in learning to   38 25
key.   Mastery of little things now is certain to make the   44 29
big jobs easier to do just right a little later.   Knowledge,   50 33
skill, and purpose are the keys to your success.   55 36

| 1 | 2 | 3 | 4 | 5 | 6 |
| 1 | 2 | 3 | 4 |

Enrichment

Technique Mastery

1. Key each line once at an easy, steady pace.
2. Key each line again at a faster pace; try to force your speed.

Figure-technique mastery (quiet hands; *finger* reaches)

1 for 494 may 617 sir 284 lap 910 rod 493 got 505 the 563 firm
2 On August 20, 1998, we moved from 3746 Oak St. to 50 Elm Ct.

3 card 3143 only 9696 fact 5135 upon 7096 case 3123 limp 98706
4 Order Nos. 56173 and 62840 must be paid no later than May 9.

5 with 2856 quay 1716 door 3994 girl 5849 flap 4910 slam 29175
6 We need to order Stock Nos. 1056, 2948, and 3746 by March 1.

Response-pattern mastery (change speed to fit word difficulty)

7 you get mop car ply far pump area null ever junk after nylon
letter response
8 you were|few ever|tax only|oil case|act upon|after you trade
9 Get him my extra tax card only after you set up a case date.

10 when also such form both with then city name than paid their
word response
11 also work|with them|paid both|they held|soap firm|such forms
12 Six of the firms may also make a bid for the city dock work.

13 the oil for you may act due him she sat did get but red wish
combination response
14 she was|the mop|for him|may get|they are|big jump|to aid the
15 Kent was to get a pump for the small oil firm on the island.

| 1 | 2 | 3 | 4 | 5 | 6 | 7 | 8 | 9 | 10 | 11 | 12 |

6C ◆ 17
New-Key Mastery

1. Key the lines once SS; DS between 2-line groups.
2. Key the lines again at a faster pace.

Technique goals
- curved, upright fingers
- finger-action keystrokes
- quiet hands/arms
- out-and-down shifting

TECHNIQUE CUE:
Eyes on copy except when you lose your place.

abbrev./ initials
1 He said ft. for feet; rd. for road; fl. for floor.
2 Lt. Hahn let L. K. take the old gong to Lake Neil.

3d row emphasis
3 Lars is to ask at the old store for a kite for Jo.
4 Ike said he is to take the old road to Lake Heidi.

key words
5 a an or he to if do it of so is go for got old led
6 go the off aid dot end jar she fit oak and had rod

key phrases
7 if so|it is|to do|if it|do so|to go|he is|to do it
8 to the|and do|is the|got it|if the|for the|ask for

all letters learned
9 Ned asked her to send the log to an old ski lodge.
10 O. J. lost one of the sleds he took off the train.

6D ◆ 5
Technique: Space Bar and Return

1. Key each line once SS; DS at end of line 7.
2. Key the drill again at a faster pace if time permits.

SPACING CUE:
Quickly strike **Space Bar** *immediately* after last letter in the word.

1 Jan is to sing.

2 Karl is at the lake.

3 Lena is to send the disk.

4 Lars is to jog to the old inn.

5 Hanna took the girls to a ski lake.

6 Hal is to take the old list to his desk.

7 Lana is to take the jar to the store at nine.

Return and start each new line quickly.

Enrichment

1. Key each line once SS; DS between 3-line groups.
2. Rekey the drill at a faster pace if time permits.

PRACTICE CUE:
In lines 4-7, keep insertion point moving steadily—no stops or pauses within the line.

Spacing/Shifting
1 K. L. Jakes is to see Lt. Hahn at Oak Lake at one.
2 Janet Harkins sent the sales sheet to Jack Hansen.
3 Karla Kent is to go to London to see Laska Jolson.

Keying easy sentences
4 Kae is to go to the lake to fish off an old skiff.
5 Joel is to ask his good friend to go to the shore.
6 Lara and her dad took eight girls for a long hike.
7 Kent said his dad is to sell the oak and ash logs.

Lesson 6

Lesson 24

Alphanumeric Keying Skills

Objectives:
1. To improve technique on individual letters.
2. To increase speed on 1', 2', and 3' writings.

24A ◆ 5
Conditioning Practice

each line once SS; DS; each line again

alphabet	1	Bonzi may pick kumquats if Jorge will drive the old ox cart.
figures	2	On August 20 we had 84 copies of T37; 95 of B16; 32 of M247.
easy	3	They work with good form and vigor to make it to their goal.

| 1 | 2 | 3 | 4 | 5 | 6 | 7 | 8 | 9 | 10 | 11 | 12 |

Skillbuilding

24B ◆ 30
Keyboard Mastery

each line once SS; DS; difficult lines again as time permits

A	1	Ada made good marks in all her classes and led her gym team.
B	2	Bubba dribbles the ball before he bounces it past the guard.
C	3	Cincy quickly cut the corn off the cob for her uncle to can.
D	4	Danny was added to the squad after an end dropped out today.
E	5	Euris felt the need to see her teacher about an oral report.
F	6	Ford left for the ski lift after a snack of fish and coffee.
G	7	Giget bought a bright green organza gown with an orange bow.
H	8	Harl feels he has had a bad time if he has had to work hard.
I	9	Iona is in line for a big raise in pay if given the new job.
J	10	Jo just jumped for joy as a judge gave her a major jury job.
K	11	Kiko asked the clerk to work quickly to check in the skiers.
L	12	Lolita will file a claim for a small parcel of my lake land.
M	13	Max may miss most of the game if the swim team misses a bus.
N	14	Nancy knew that her son had gone to the tennis court at ten.
O	15	Ossido opted to go to the opera instead of the opening game.
P	16	Patsy has put too much pepper in the soup pot for my palate.
Q	17	Quade uses quick quiet quips to quell squash squad quarrels.
R	18	Rosa read her story to thirty rapt students in third period.
S	19	Steve said his plans to improve the system met with success.
T	20	Tricia said to take a little time for thought before we act.
U	21	Uri quickly turned our bus around and drove up the mountain.
V	22	Viv used vim and vigor to have voters approve a savings tax.
W	23	Walter now wants to write news items for a weekly news show.
X	24	Xenia next faxed us six tax bills as extra extreme examples.
Y	25	Yancy saw your yellow yacht motor by a buoy in a nearby bay.
Z	26	Zelda, gazing at a hazy horizon, was puzzled by fuzzy ships.

Lesson 24

Review

RA◆ 8

Conditioning Practice

each line twice SS (slowly, then faster); DS between 2-line groups; if time permits, practice each line again

Space once.

reach review	1 ik rf ol ed nj gf hj tf .l ft. i.e. e.g. rt. J. L.
spacing	2 a an go is or to if he and got the for led kit lot
left shift	3 I got it. Hal has it. Jan led Nan. Kae is gone.

RB◆ 8

Keyboard Mastery

each line once SS; DS between 2-line groups; QS at end of drill

Technique goals
- curved, upright fingers
- wrists low, but not resting
- quick-snap keystrokes
- finger reaches; hands and arms steady

h/e	1 hj ed jhj ded ha el he she led had eke hal ale die
	2 Heidi had a good lead at the end of the first set.
	DS
i/r	3 ik rf kik frf is or sir ire ore his risk fire ride
	4 Kier is taking a high risk if he rides that horse.
	DS
o/t	5 ol tf lol ftf so it of too oft hot toe lot the old
	6 Ola has lost the list she took to that food store.
	DS
n/g	7 nj gf jnj fgf go an got and nag gin hang gone sign
	8 Lang and she are going to sing nine songs at noon.
	DS
left shift/.	9 Oak Lake; N. J. Karis; Lt. L. J. Oates; Lara Nador
	10 J. K. Larkin is going to Idaho to see Linda Jakes.

RC◆ 4

Technique: Return

each line once SS; DS between 2-line groups

RETURN CUE:
Keep your pace to the end of the line; return immediately; start the new line without pausing.

1 Nan has gone to ski;
2 she took a train at nine.

Keep eyes on copy as you return.

3 Janet asked for the disk;
4 she is to take it to the lake.

5 Karl said he left at the lake
6 a file that has the data she needs.

7 Nadia said she felt ill as the ski
8 lift left to take the girls to the hill.

23C ◆ 15

Speed Building: Guided Writing

1. Key one 1' unguided and two 1' guided writings on ¶ 1 and then on ¶ 2.
2. Key two 2' unguided writings on ¶s 1-2 combined; find *gwam* on each.
3. Key a 3' writing on ¶s 1-2 combined; find *gwam*.

1' *gwam* goals

▽ 23 = acceptable
⊡ 27 = average
⊙ 31 = good
◇ 35 = excellent

The **la** above these ¶s shows that they are low average difficulty—a bit more difficult than the ¶s in previous lessons.

la   all letters used   2' | 3'

When saying hello to someone is the correct thing to do,   6 | 4
make direct eye contact and greet the person with vitality   12 | 8
in your voice. Do not look down or away or speak only in a   18 | 12
whisper. Make the person feel happy for having seen you, and 24 | 16
you will feel much better about yourself as a consequence.   30 | 20

Similarly, when you shake hands with another person,   35 | 23
look that person in the eye and offer a firm but not crushing 41 | 27
shake of the hand. Just a firm shake or two will do.   Next   47 | 31
time you meet a new person, do not puzzle about whether to   53 | 35
shake hands.   Quickly offer your firm hand with confidence.   59 | 39

| 1 | 2 | 3 | 4 | 5 | 6 |
| 1 | 2 | 3 | 4 |

Enrichment

Technique Mastery

1. Key each line once at an easy, steady pace.
2. Key each line again at a faster pace; try to force your speed.

Figure-technique mastery (quiet hands; *finger* reaches)

1 it 85 do 39 if 84 so 29 an 16 am 17 of 94 us 72 go 50 he 630
2 I was 17 on May 20, 1998; 6 ft. tall; weighed 153 lbs. 4 oz.

3 as 12 we 23 up 70 in 86 at 15 no 69 be 53 on 96 ax 12 re 433
4 In our last 3 games we won 60 to 54, 71 to 69, and 52 to 38.

5 make 7183 kept 8305 work 2948 half 6194 gush 5726 fish 48263
6 Key these numbers: 305, 1492, 1776, 1862, 1914, 1929, 1946.

Response-pattern mastery (change speed to fit word difficulty)

letter response
7 a in be on we up as my at no was you are him get few see set
8 at no| as my| on you| we are| get him| at best| in fact| as you saw
9 As you see, you are free only after you get a case date set.

word response
10 of is it he to by or us an so if do am go me the six and but
11 to me| of us| and may| pay for| big box| the six| but due| own them
12 The city is to pay for the field work both men did for them.

combination response
13 of we to in or on is be it as by no if at us up an my he was
14 is in| if we do| is up to| may get all| she was off| pay you then
15 Tish saw you sign the tax form after you paid the city fees.

| 1 | 2 | 3 | 4 | 5 | 6 | 7 | 8 | 9 | 10 | 11 | 12 |

RD◆ 10
Technique: Space Bar and Left Shift

each line twice SS; DS between 2-line groups

Goals
- to reduce the pause between words
- to reduce the time taken to shift/strike key/release when making capital letters

Down-and-in spacing

Out-and-down shifting

Upright fingers

Space Bar (Space *immediately* after each word.)

1 if is an he go is or ah to of so it do el id la ti

2 an el | go to | if he | of it | is to | do the | for it | and so

3 if she is | it is the | all of it | go to the | for an oak

Left Shift key (Shift; strike key; release both quickly.)

4 Lt. Ho said he left the skiff at Ord Lake for her.

5 Jane or Hal is to go to Lake Heed to see Kate Orr.

6 O. J. Halak is to ask for her at Jahn Hall at one.

RE◆ 20
Speed Building

each line twice SS (slowly, then faster); DS between 2-line groups

Correct finger curvature

Correct finger alignment

Key words (*Think*, *say*, and *key* the words.)

1 an the did oak she for off tie got and led jar all

2 go end air her dog his aid rid sit and fir ask jet

3 talk side jell gold fled sign stir fork high shall

Key phrases (*Think*, *say*, and *key* the phrases.)

4 to do | it is | of an | if he | is to | or do | to it | if he is

5 to aid | if she | he did | of the | to all | is for | is a tie

6 is to ask | is to aid | he or she | to rig it | if she did

Key sentences (Strike keys at a brisk, steady pace.)

7 Joan is to go to the lake to get her old red skis.

8 Les asked for a list of all the old gold she sold.

9 Laska said she left the old disk list on his desk.

Lessons 23-24

Master Alphanumeric Keyboarding Technique
Lesson 23 Alphanumeric Keying Skills

Objectives:
1. To improve technique on individual letters.
2. To improve keying speed on 1', 2', and 3' writings.

23A♦ 5
Conditioning Practice

each line twice SS; then a 1'
writing on line 3; find *gwam*

alphabet	1	Lopez knew our squad could just slip by the next five games.
figures	2	Check Numbers 267, 298, 304, and 315 were still outstanding.
easy	3	Dixie works with vigor to make the theory work for a profit.

| 1 | 2 | 3 | 4 | 5 | 6 | 7 | 8 | 9 | 10 | 11 | 12 |

Skillbuilding

23B♦ 30
**Technique Mastery:
Individual Letters**

1. Key each line twice SS; DS between 2-line groups. Note the lines that were difficult for you.
2. Key those lines again.

Technique goals
- curved, upright fingers
- quick-snap keystrokes
- quiet hands and arms

A	1	Ana ate a salami sandwich and some papaya after a quick nap.
B	2	Bobby bought a beach ball and big balloons for the big bash.
C	3	Cora can serve cake and coffee to the cold campers at lunch.
D	4	David did all he could to dazzle the crowd with wild dances.
E	5	Elaine left her new sled in an old shed near the grey house.
F	6	Frank found a file folder his father had left in the office.
G	7	Gloria got the giggles when the juggler dropped his oranges.
H	8	Hugh helped his big brother haul in the fishing net for her.
I	9	Inez sings in a trio that is part of a big choir at college.
J	10	Jason just joined the jury to judge the major jazz festival.
K	11	Kurt makes kapok pillows for kayaks and ketches at the dock.
L	12	Lola left her doll collection for a village gallery to sell.
M	13	Myna asked her mom to make more malted milk for the mission.
N	14	Nadine knew her aunt made lemonade and sun tea this morning.
O	15	Owen took the book from the shelf to copy his favorite poem.
P	16	Pamela added a pinch of pepper and paprika to a pot of soup.
Q	17	Quent posed quick quiz questions to his quiet croquet squad.
R	18	Risa used a rubber raft to rescue four girls from the river.
S	19	Silas said his sister has won six medals in just four meets.
T	20	Trisha told a tall tale about three little kittens in a tub.
U	21	Ursula asked the usual questions about four issues you face.
V	22	Vinny voted for five very vital issues of value to everyone.
W	23	Wilt wants to walk in the walkathon next week and show well.
X	24	Xania next expects them to fix the extra fax machine by six.
Y	25	Yuri said your yellow yacht was the envy of every yachtsman.
Z	26	Zoella and a zany friend ate a sizzling pizza in the piazza.

L e s s o n   7

New Keys: U and C

O b j e c t i v e s :

1. **To learn reach technique for U and C.**
2. **To combine smoothly U and C with all other learned keys.**

7A◆   8

Conditioning Practice

each line twice SS (slowly, then faster); DS between 2-line groups

reach review 1 nj gf ol rf ik ed .l tf hj fr ki ft jn de lo fg l.

space bar 2 an do in so to go fan hen log gin tan son not sign

left shift 3 Olga has the first slot; Jena is to skate for her.

7B◆   20

New Keys: U and C

each line twice SS (slowly, then faster); DS between 2-line groups; if time permits, repeat lines 7-9

u *Right index* finger

c *Left middle* finger

Follow the *Standard Plan for Learning New Keys* outlined on p. 8.

Learn u

1 j j uj uj us us us jug jug jut jut due due fur fur

2 uj uj jug jug sue sue lug lug use use lug lug dues

3 a jug; due us; the fur; use it; a fur rug; is just

Learn c

4 d d cd cd cod cod cog cog tic tic cot cot can cans

5 cd cd cod cod ice ice can can code code dock docks

6 a cod; a cog; the ice; she can; the dock; the code

Combine u and c

7 cud cud cut cuts cur curs cue cues duck ducks clue

8 a cud; a cur; to cut; the cue; the cure; for luck;

9 use a clue; a fur coat; take the cue; cut the cake

Skillbuilding

22D◆   8
Technique: Keying, Spacing, Shifting

1. Key each line once SS; DS between 2-line groups.
2. Key a 1' writing on line 7 and then on line 8 if time permits; find *gwam* on each.

quick-snap keystrokes
1 Ella may go to the soap firm for title to all the lake land.
2 Did the bugle corps toot with the usual vigor for the queen?

down-and-in spacing
3 Coy is in the city to buy an oak chair he wants for his den.
4 Jan may go to town by bus to sign a work form for a new job.

out-and-down shifting
5 Robb and Ty are in Madrid to spend a week with Jae and Aldo.
6 Are you going in May, or in June? Elena is leaving in July.

easy
7 Rick paid for both the visual aid and the sign for the firm.
8 Glena kept all the work forms on the shelf by the big chair.

| 1 | 2 | 3 | 4 | 5 | 6 | 7 | 8 | 9 | 10 | 11 | 12 |

22E◆   12
Speed Check

line spacing: DS
1. Key two 1' writings on each ¶; find *gwam* on each writing.
2. Key a 2' writing on ¶s 1-2 combined; find *gwam*.
3. Key a 3' writing on ¶s 1-2 combined; find *gwam*.

Goals
1': At least 24 *gwam*.
2': At least 23 *gwam*.
3': At least 22 *gwam*.

e   all letters used   2' | 3'

Success does not mean the same thing to everyone. For   6 | 4
some, it means to get to the top at all costs: in power, in   12 | 8
fame, and in income. For others, it means just to fulfill   18 | 12
their basic needs or wants with as little effort as required.   24 | 16

Most people fall within the two extremes. They work quite   30 | 20
hard to better their lives at home, at work, and in the social   36 | 24
world. They realize that success for them is not in being at   42 | 28
the top but rather in trying to improve their quality of life.   48 | 32

| 1 | 2 | 3 | 4 | 5 | 6 |
| 1 | 2 | 3 | 4 |

Enrichment

Proofreading

1. Print the 3' writing you keyed in 22E.
2. Note the kinds of errors marked in the ¶ at right.
3. Note how proofreader's marks above the copy are used to mark errors for correction.
4. Proofread the printout of your 3' writing; mark each error for correction, using proofreader's marks.

= space   **∧** = insert   **⌒** = close up   **⌿** = delete   **∿** = transpose (tr)

Sucess ① does not mean the#same ② thing to every⌒one ③. For some,
it means to get to ① the top att ② all costs: in power, in fame, and
in income ①. For others, ② it means juts ③ to fulfill their basic needs
or of ① wants with ② as little effort ∧required ③.

Line 1	Line 2	Line 3	Line 4
1 Omitted letter	1 Omitted word	1 Misstroke	1 Added word
2 Failure to space	2 Added letter	2 Omitted comma	2 Transposition
3 Faulty spacing	3 Faulty spacing	3 Transposition	3 Omitted word

Lesson 22

7C◆   17
New-Key Mastery

1. Key the lines once SS; DS between 2-line groups.
2. Key the lines again at a faster pace.

Technique goals

■ reach up without moving hands away from you

■ reach down without moving hands toward your body

■ use quick-snap keystrokes

3d/1st rows	1	in cut nut ran cue can cot fun hen car urn den cog
	2	Nan is cute; he is curt; turn a cog; he can use it
left shift and .	3	Kae had taken a lead. Jack then cut ahead of her.
	4	I said to use Kan. for Kansas and Ore. for Oregon.
key words	5	and cue for jut end kit led old fit just golf coed
	6	an due cut such fuss rich lack turn dock turf curl
key phrases	7	an urn|is due|to cut|for us|to use|cut off|such as
	8	just in|code it|turn on|cure it|as such|is in luck
all keys learned	9	Nida is to get the ice; Jacki is to call for cola.
	10	Ira is sure that he can go there in an hour or so.

7D◆   5
Technique: Space Bar and Left Shift

Key the lines once SS; DS between 3-line groups. Keep hand movement to a minimum.

	1	Ken said he is to sign the list and take the disk.
space bar	2	It is right for her to take the lei if it is hers.
	3	Jae has gone to see an old oaken desk at the sale.
	4	He said to enter Oh. for Ohio and Kan. for Kansas.
left shift	5	It is said that Lt. Li has an old jet at Lake Ida.
	6	L. N. is at the King Hotel; Harl is at the Leland.

Enrichment

1. Key each line once SS; DS between 2-line groups.
2. If time permits, key the lines again at a faster pace.

PRACTICE CUE:

Try to reduce hand movement and the tendency of unused fingers to fly out or follow reaching finger.

u/c	1	uj cd uc juj dcd cud cut use cog cue urn curl luck
	2	Huck can use the urn for the social at the church.
n/g	3	nj gf nj gin can jog nick sign nigh snug rung clog
	4	Nan can jog to the large sign at the old lake gin.
all keys learned	5	nj gf uj cd ol tf ik rf hj ed an go or is to he .l
	6	Leona has gone to ski; Jack had left here at nine.
all keys learned	7	an or is to he go cue for and jak she all use curt
	8	Nick sells jade rings; Jahn got one for good luck.

Lesson 7

Lesson 22

New Keys: 6 and 2

Objectives:
1. To learn the reach technique for 6 and 2.
2. To improve/assess skill on straight-copy sentences/paragraphs.

22A◆ 5
Conditioning Practice

line spacing: SS
side margins: default
each line twice; DS between 2-line groups; then a 1' writing on line 3

alphabet 1 Jared helped Mazy quickly fix the big wood stove in the den.

figures 2 Bella lives at 1847 Oak Street; Jessi, at 5039 Duard Circle.

easy 3 They may make their goals if they work with the usual vigor.

| 1 | 2 | 3 | 4 | 5 | 6 | 7 | 8 | 9 | 10 | 11 | 12 |

22B◆ 18
New Keys: 6 and 2

each line twice (slowly, then faster); DS between 2-line groups; if time permits, key lines 5-8 again

6 *Right index* finger

2 *Left ring* finger

Follow the *Standard Plan for Learning New Keys* outlined on p. 8.

Learn 6

1 j j 6j 6j jj 66 j6j j6j 66j 66j Reach up for 6, 66, and 666.
2 Key the figures 6, 66, and 666. Did just 6 of 66 finish it?

Learn 2

3 s s 2s 2s ss 22 s2s s2s 22s 22s Reach up for 2, 22, and 222.
4 Add the figures 2, 22, and 222. Review pages 2 to 22 today.

Combine 6, 2, and other figures

5 Key 22, 26, 62, and 66. Just 22 of the 66 scouts were here.
6 Reach with the fingers to key 26 and 262 as well as 2 and 6.

7 Key figures as units: 18, 26, 37, 49, 50, 62, 162, and 268.
8 The proxy dated April 26, 1997, was vital in Case No. 30584.

22C◆ 7
New-Key Mastery

each line once SS

1 Lee has sold 16 elm, 28 ash, 37 oak, 49 pine, and 50 shrubs.

2 Flights 201 and 384 will be replaced by Flights 625 and 749.

3 Key as a unit: 10, 29, 38, 47, 56; two units, 162 and 4837.

4 In 1996, 26 of our 384 workers were moved to 507 Pecos Lane.

New Keys: W and Right Shift

Objectives:
1. **To learn reach technique for W and Right Shift.**
2. **To combine smoothly W and Right Shift with other learned keys.**

8A◆   8

Conditioning Practice

each line twice SS (slowly, then faster); DS between 2-line groups

reach review 1 a;sldkfj a;sldkfj uj cd ik rf nj ed hj tf ol gf .1

u/c 2 us cod use cut sue cot jut cog nut cue con lug ice

all letters learned 3 Hugh has just taken a lead in a race for a record.

8B◆   20

New Keys: W and Right Shift

each line twice SS (slowly, then faster); DS between 2-line groups; if time permits, rekey lines 7-9

w *Left ring* finger

Right Shift *Right little* finger

SHIFTING CUE:
Shift, strike key, and release both in a quick 1-2-3 count.

Follow the *Standard Plan for Learning New Keys* outlined on p. 8.

Learn w

1 s s ws ws sow sow wow wow low low how how cow cows

2 sw sw ws ws ow ow now now row row own own tow tows

3 to sow; is how; so low; to own; too low; is to row

Learn Right Shift key

4 A; A; Al Al; Cal Cal; Ali or Flo; Di and Sol left.

5 Ali lost to Ron; Cal lost to Elsa; Di lost to Del.

6 Tina has left for Tucson; Dori can find her there.

Combine w and Right Shift

7 Dodi will ask if Willa went to Town Center at two.

8 Wilf left the show for which he won a Gower Award.

9 Walt will go to Rio on a golf tour with Wolf Towe.

Skillbuilding

21D ◆ 8
Speed Check

line spacing: DS

1. Key a 1' writing on ¶ 1 and then on ¶ 2; find *gwam* on each ¶.
2. Key two 2' writings on ¶s 1-2 together; find *gwam* on each writing.

1' *gwam* goals

▽ 21 = acceptable
⊡ 25 = average
⊙ 29 = good
◇ 33 = excellent

e all letters used

Time and motion are major items in building our keying   6
power. As we make each move through space to a letter or a   12
figure, we use time. So we want to be sure that every move   18
is quick and direct. We cut time and aid speed in this way.   24

A good way to reduce motion and thus save time is just   29
to keep the hands in home position as you make the reach to   35
a letter or figure. Fix your gaze on the copy; then, reach   41
to each key with a direct, low move at your very best speed.   47

| 1 | 2 | 3 | 4 | 5 | 6 |

21E ◆ 12
Technique Mastery

1. Key each line once at an easy, steady pace; try to improve your technique.
2. Key each line again; try to increase your speed.

TECHNIQUE CUES:

- space quickly with down-and-in motion
- shift without moving hands down or elbows in or out
- keep fingers upright (not slanting) on home keys
- adjust speed to fit difficulty of words

Spacing

1 an am by pan ham any born slam gory then them they torn slam
2 I am|is on|go by|if any|by then|of them|is torn|if they sign
3 Stan is to go by the inn to sign the work form for the firm.

Shifting

4 Janette or Spiro|Apps and Kahn|J. A. Wolf Co.|March or April
5 FBLA meets on Tuesday, January 18, in Room 39 of Mason Hall.
6 Marvel and Sons is to build Fair Oaks Center on Sparks Lake.

Adjacent keys

7 rent sail mask riot last trim fort coin stop port more ruins
8 we try|as rent|we knew|her last|has more|new coin|mere hopes
9 Hoping that her old coins were a real buy, we made an offer.

Response patterns

10 so we if as pen was may far lay gas firm plum make gear with

combination response

11 if we|so as|the mop|may set|and get|they jump|she was to pay
12 He was to see if the dock crew was paid a good rate to work.

| 1 | 2 | 3 | 4 | 5 | 6 | 7 | 8 | 9 | 10 | 11 | 12 |

Lesson 21

LEARN 7 AND 3

57

8C ◆ 17
New-Key Mastery

1. Key the lines once SS; DS between 2-line groups.
2. Key the lines again at a faster pace.

Goal: finger-action reaches; quiet hands and arms

w and right shift
1 Dr. Rowe is in Tulsa now; Dr. Cowan will see Rolf.
2 Gwinn took the gown to Golda Swit on Downs Circle.

n/g
3 to go|go on|no go|an urn|dug in|and got|and a sign
4 He is to sign for the urn to go on the high chest.

key words
5 if ow us or go he an it of own did oak the cut jug
6 do all and for cog odd ant fig rug low cue row end

key phrases
7 we did|for a jar|she is due|cut the oak|he owns it
8 all of us|to own the|she is to go|when he has gone

all keys learned
9 Jan and Chris are gone; Di and Nick get here soon.
10 Doug will work for her at the new store in Newton.

8D ◆ 5
Technique: Spacing with Punctuation

each line once DS

No space   **Space once.**

1 Use i.e. for that is; cs. for case; ck. for check.
2 Dr. Wong said to use wt. for weight; in. for inch.
3 R. D. Roth has used ed. for editor; Rt. for Route.
4 Wes said Ed Rowan got an Ed.D. degree last winter.

Enrichment

1. Key each pair of lines once SS.
2. Key each even-numbered line again to increase speed.

Technique goals
- steady hands/arms
- finger-action keystrokes
- unused fingers curved, upright over home keys
- eyes on copy as you key

u/c
1 uj cd uc cut cut cue cue use use cod cod dock dock
2 Jud is to cut the corn near the dock for his aunt.

w and right shift
3 Don and Willa|Dot or Wilda|R. W. Gowan|Dr. Wilford
4 Dr. Wold will set the wrist of Sgt. Wills at noon.

left shift and .
5 Jane or Har|Jae and Nan|L. N. Hagel|Lt. J. O. Hao
6 Lt. Hawser said that he will see us in New London.

n/g
7 nj gf ng gun gun nag nag got got nor nor sign sign
8 Angie hung a huge sign in front of the union hall.

o/t
9 ol tf to too dot dot not not toe toe got goat goat
10 Todd took the tool chest to the dock for a worker.

i/r
11 ik rf or ore fir fir sir sir ire ire ice ice irons
12 Risa fired the fir log to heat rice for the girls.

h/e
13 hj ed he the the hen hen when when then then their
14 He was with her when she chose her new snow shoes.

L e s s o n 2 1

New Keys: 7 and 3

21A◆   5
Conditioning Practice
line spacing: SS
side margins: default

each line twice; DS between 2-line groups; then a 1' writing on line 3

alphabet 1 Gavin made a quick fall trip by jet to Zurich six weeks ago.
figures 2 Key 1 and 4 and 5 and 8 and 9 and 0 and 190 and 504 and 958.
easy 3 The man is to fix the big sign by the field for a city firm.

| 1 | 2 | 3 | 4 | 5 | 6 | 7 | 8 | 9 | 10 | 11 | 12 |

21B◆   18
New Keys: 7 and 3

each line twice SS (slowly, then faster); DS between 2-line groups; if time permits, key lines 5-7 again

Follow the *Standard Plan for Learning New Keys* outlined on p. 8.

7 *Right index* finger

3 *Left middle* finger

Learn 7

1 j j 7j 7j jj 77 j7j j7j 77j 77j Reach up for 7, 77, and 777.
2 Key the figures 7, 77, and 777.   She checked Rooms 7 and 77.

Learn 3

3 d d 3d 3d dd 33 d3d d3d 33d 33d Reach up for 3, 33, and 333.
4 Add the figures 3, 33, and 333.   Read pages 3 to 33 tonight.

Combine 7 and 3

5 Key 33, 37, 73, and 77.   Just 37 of the 77 skiers have come.
6 Please order 7 Model 337 computers and 3 Model 737 printers.
7 On August 7, the 33 bikers left on a long trip of 377 miles.

Skillbuilding

21C◆   7
Technique:
Response Patterns

1. Key each pair of lines once SS; DS between 2-line groups.
2. Key a 1' writing on line 2 and then on line 4; find *gwam* on each. Rekey the slower line if time permits.

letter response 1 face pump ever milk area jump vast only save upon safe union
2 As we were in a junk, we saw a rare loon feast on a crawdad.

word response 3 quay hand also body lend hang mane down envy risk corn whale
4 Tisha is to go to the lake with us if she is to do the work.

combination response 5 with only | they join | half safe | born free | firm look | goal rates
6 I sat on the airy lanai with my gaze on the sea to the east.

| 1 | 2 | 3 | 4 | 5 | 6 | 7 | 8 | 9 | 10 | 11 | 12 |

Lesson 9

New Keys: B and Y

Objectives:
1. To learn reach technique for B and Y.
2. To combine smoothly B and Y with all other learned keys.

Fingers curved

Fingers upright

9A◆   7
Conditioning Practice

each line twice SS (slowly, then faster); DS between 2-line groups

reach review 1 uj ws ik rf ol cd nj ed hj tf .l gf sw ju de lo fr

c/n 2 an can and cut end cue hen cog torn dock then sick

all letters learned 3 A kid had a jag of fruit on his cart in New Delhi.

9B◆   5
Technique: Space Bar

each line once

Technique goal
Space with a down-and-in motion *immediately* after each word.

1 He will take an old urn to an art sale at the inn.

2 Ann has an old car she wants to sell at this sale.

3 Len is to work for us for a week at the lake dock.

4 Gwen is to sign for the auto we set aside for her.

5 Jan is in town for just one week to look for work.

6 Juan said he was in the auto when it hit the tree.

9C◆   4
Technique: Return

1. Key each line once SS: return and start each new line quickly.
2. On line 4, see how many words you can key in 30 seconds (30"). The count-down timer in *MicroType Pro* (*MicroType Multimedia*) is available for this purpose. See p. xiii.

1 Dot is to go at two.

2 He saw that it was a good law.

3 Rilla is to take the auto into the town.

4 Wilt has an old gold jug he can enter in the show.

| 1 | 2 | 3 | 4 | 5 | 6 | 7 | 8 | 9 | 10 |

A **standard word** in keyboarding is 5 characters or any combination of 5 characters and spaces, as indicated by the number scale under line 4 above. The number of standard words keyed in 1' is called gross words a minute (*gwam*).

To find 1-minute (1') *gwam:*
1. Note on the scale the figure beneath the last word you keyed. That is your 1' *gwam* if you keyed the line partially or only once in 1'.

2. If you completed the line once and started over, add the figure determined in Step 1 to the figure 10. The resulting figure is your 1' *gwam*.

To find 30-second (30") *gwam:*
1. Find 1' *gwam* (total words keyed in 1').
2. Multiply 1' *gwam* by 2. The resulting figure is your 30" *gwam*.

20D◆ 12
Skill Transfer: Straight Copy, Script, Rough Draft

1. Key each ¶ once SS; DS between ¶s.
2. Key a 1' writing on each ¶; find *gwam* on each writing; compare the three rates.
3. Key one or two more 1' writings on the two slowest ¶s to improve skill transfer.

Your *gwam* on script will be lower than your rate on straight copy; your *gwam* on rough draft likely will be still lower. Improving skill transfer means trying to close the gap between your straight-copy *gwam* and the other rates, though the rates will rarely be the same.

Proofreader's Marks

stet	= no change
∧	= insert
⨍	= delete
#	= add space
◯	= close up
∽	= transpose
⊙	= insert period

Straight copy 1'

It is up to you to proofread the copy you produce to 11
find any mistakes you may have made. It is also up to you 22
to correct all the errors you find if the copy is to serve 34
a purpose other than to show that you have done the work. 46

| 1 | 2 | 3 | 4 | 5 | 6 | 7 | 8 | 9 | 10 | 11 | 12 |

Script

It is vital to check your copy word for word against 11
the source copy from which you keyed. The words should 22
be in the same order, and each word must be spelled right. 34
A space should be left after each word or punctuation mark. 46

Rough draft

Be quick to discover your errors even if you will not 11
correct them just now. As soon as you begin to apply your 22
skill you may be taught easy ways to correct errors. For now, 35
learn to excel in marking and finding them. 44

20E◆ 10
Speed Building

1. Key a 1' unguided and a 1' *guided* writing on each ¶ (see p. 45 for procedure).
2. Key a 2' writing on ¶s 1-2 together; find *gwam* for each writing.

e all letters used 2'

•   2   •   4   •   6   •   8   •   10   •
I am now trying to learn to vary my keying rate to fit 5
12   •   14   •   16   •   18   •   20   •   22   •
the job of keying the words. When I learn to speed up more 11
24   •   26   •   28   •   30   •   32   •   34   •
of the easy words, I can take time to break the longer ones 17
36   •   38   •   40   •   42   •
into small parts and handle them quickly. 22

•   2   •   4   •   6   •   8   •   10   •
With a bit more practice, I shall be able to handle by 27
12   •   14   •   16   •   18   •   20   •   22   •
word response more of the shorter ones that just now I must 33
24   •   26   •   28   •   30   •   32   •   34   •
analyze and key letter by letter. As I learn to do more of 39
36   •   38   •   40   •   42   •   44   •
these words as units, I shall become more expert. 44

| 1 | 2 | 3 | 4 | 5 | 6 |

9D◆ 19
New Keys: B and Y

each line twice SS (slowly, then faster): DS between 2-line groups; QS between groupings; if time permits, rekey lines 7-9

b *Left index* finger

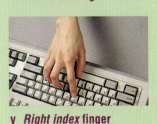

y *Right index* finger

Follow the *Standard Plan for Learning New Keys* outlined on p. 8.

Learn b
1 f f bf bf fib fib rob rob but but big big fib fibs
2 bf bf rob rob lob lob orb orb bid bid bud bud ribs
3 a rib; to fib; rub it; an orb; or rob; but she bid

Learn y
4 j j yj yj jay jay lay lay hay hay day day say says
5 yj yj jay jay eye eye dye dye yes yes yet yet jays
6 a jay; to say; an eye; he says; dye it; has an eye

Combine b and y
7 by by buy buy boy boy bye bye byte byte buoy buoys
8 by it; to buy; by you; a byte; the buoy; by and by
9 Jaye went by bus to the store to buy the big buoy.

9E◆ 15
New-Key Mastery

1. Key the lines once SS; DS between 2-line groups.
2. Key the lines again at a faster pace.

PRACTICE CUES:
- reach *up* without moving hands away from you
- reach *down* without moving hands toward your body
- use quick-snap keystrokes

reach review
1 a;sldkfj bf ol ed yj ws ik rf hj cd nj tf .l gf uj
2 a kit low for jut led sow fob ask sun cud jet grow

3d/1st rows
3 no in bow any tub yen cut sub coy ran bin cow deck
4 Cody wants to buy this baby cub for the young boy.

key words
5 by and for the got all did but cut now say jut ask
6 work just such hand this goal boys held furl eight

key phrases
7 to do|can go|to bow|for all|did jet|ask her|to buy
8 if she|to work|and such|the goal|for this|held the

all letters learned
9 Becky has auburn hair and wide eyes of light jade.
10 Juan left Bobby at the dog show near our ice rink.

| 1 | 2 | 3 | 4 | 5 | 6 | 7 | 8 | 9 | 10 |

Lesson 9

Lesson 20

New Keys: 0 and 5

Objectives:

1. To learn reach technique for 0 and 5.
2. To improve technique/speed on straight-copy sentences/paragraphs.

20A◆ 5

Conditioning Practice

line spacing: SS
side margins: default

each line twice (slowly, then faster); DS between 2-line groups; then a 1' writing on line 3

alphabet 1 Roz may put a vivid sign next to the low aqua boat for Jack.

figures 2 Please review Figure 8 on page 94 and Figure 14 on page 189.

easy 3 Tien may fix the bus panel for the city if the pay is right.

| 1 | 2 | 3 | 4 | 5 | 6 | 7 | 8 | 9 | 10 | 11 | 12 |

20B◆ 18

New Keys: 0 and 5

each line twice (slowly, then faster); DS between 2-line groups; if time permits, key lines 5-7 again

0 *Right little* finger

5 *Left index* finger

Follow the *Standard Plan for Learning New Keys* outlined on p. 8.

Learn 0 (zero)

1 ; ; 0; 0; ;; 00 ;0; ;0; 00; 00; Reach up for 0, 00, and 000.
2 Snap the finger off the 0. I used 0, 00, and 000 sandpaper.

Learn 5

3 f f 5f 5f ff 55 f5f f5f 55f 55f Reach up for 5, 55, and 555.
4 Reach up to 5 and back to f. Did he say to order 55 or 555?

Combine 0 and 5

5 Reach with the fingers to key 50 and 500 as well as 5 and 0.
6 We asked for prices on these models: 50, 55, 500, and 5500.
7 On May 5, I got 5 boxes each of 0 and 00 steel wool for her.

20C◆ 5

New-Key Mastery

each line once DS (2 hard returns between lines)

LANGUAGE SKILLS CUES:

- No space is left before or after : when used with figures to express time.
- Most nouns before numbers are capitalized; exceptions include *page* and *line*.

No space

1 Flight 1049 is on time; it should be at Gate 48 at 5:50 p.m.
2 The club meeting on April 5 will be in Room 549 at 8:10 a.m.
3 Of our 108 workers in 1994, 14 had gone to new jobs by 1995.
4 I used Chapter 19, pages 449 to 458, for my March 10 report.
5 Can you meet us at 1954 Maple Avenue at 8:05 a.m. August 10?
6 Of the 59 students, 18 keyed at least 40 w.a.m. by April 18.

Review

O b j e c t i v e s :

1. **To improve spacing, shifting, and returning.**
2. **To increase keying control and speed.**

Before you begin each practice session:

- Position your body directly in front of the keyboard; sit erect, with feet on the floor for balance.
- Curve your fingers deeply and place them in an upright position over the home keys.
- Rest the book on the easel.

Body properly positioned

Fingers properly curved

Fingers properly upright

RA◆ 7
Conditioning Practice

each line twice SS (slowly, then faster); DS between 2-line groups; if time permits, practice each line again

reach review 1 we ok at in be on by re no us if la do ah go C. J.

b/y 2 by rub jay fib lay rob hay big say buy boy yet but

all letters learned 3 Fran knew it was her job to guide your gold truck.

RB◆ 13
Technique: Space Bar and Shift Keys

1. Key the lines once SS; DS between 2-line groups.
2. Key lines again at a faster pace.

Down-and-in spacing

Out-and-down shifting

Space bar (Space *immediately* after each word.)

1 an by win buy den sly won they than flay when clay
2 in a way | on a day | buy a hen | a fine day | if they win

3 Jay can bid on the old clay urn he saw at the inn.
4 I know she is to be here soon to talk to the club.

Shift keys (Shift; strike key; release both quickly.)

5 Lt. Su; Nan and Dodi; Karl and Sol; Dr. O. C. Goya
6 Kara and Rod are in Italy; Jane and Bo go in June.

7 Sig and Bodie went to the lake with Cory and Lana.
8 Aida Rios and Jana Hardy work for us in Los Gatos.

Script and Rough-Draft Copy

line spacing: DS
side margins: default

1. Key each line once DS (2 hard returns between lines).
2. Rekey the rough-draft lines if time permits.

Proofreader's Marks

☰	= capitalize
⋏	= insert
⋏	= delete
∏	= transpose
⋏#	= delete space
#	= add space
lc	= lowercase
◠	= close up

Script

1 Proofread: Compare copy word for word with the original.
2 Compare all figures digit by digit with your source copy.
3 Be sure to check for spacing and punctuation marks, also.
4 Copy in script or rough draft may not show exact spacing
5 It is your job to insert correct spacing as you key copy.
6 Soon you will learn how to correct your errors on screen.

Rough draft

7 cap the first word an all proper nouns in every sentence.
8 For example: pablo Mendez is from San juan, Puerto rico.
9 Ami Qwan and parents will return to Taipie this summer.
10 our coffee is from Columbia; tea, from England or china.
11 How many of you have Ethnic origins ina foreign country?
12 Did you know which of the states once were part of mexico?

Speed Building

1. Key a 1' unguided writing on each ¶. Then key a 1' *guided* writing on each ¶ (see p. 45 for procedure).
2. Key a 2' writing on ¶s 1-2 together; find *gwam*.

Quarter-Minute Checkpoints

gwam	1/4'	1/2'	3/4'	Time
16	4	8	12	16
20	5	10	15	20
24	6	12	18	24
28	7	14	21	28
32	8	16	24	32
36	9	18	27	36
40	10	20	30	40

e all letters used   2'

How much time does it take you to return at the end of   6
the line? Do you return with a lazy or a quick reach? Try   12
not to stop at the end of the line; instead, return quickly   18
and move down to the next line of copy.   21

How much time does it take you to strike the shift key   27
and the letter to make a capital? Just a bit more practice   33
will help you cut by half the time you are now using. When   39
you cut the time, you increase your speed.   43

| 1 | 2 | 3 | 4 | 5 | 6 |

RC ◆ 15

Speed Building

1. Key the lines once SS; DS between 2-line groups.
2. Key the lines again at a faster pace.

Technique goals
- curved, upright fingers
- quiet hands/arms
- quick spacing—no pause between words
- finger-reach action to shift keys

Finger-action keystrokes

Down-and-in thumb motion

Key words and phrases (*Think*, *say*, and *key* words and phrases.)

```
1 by dig row off but and jet oak the cub all got rid
2 ah she own dug irk buy cog job for yet ask led urn

3 of us|if the|all of|and do|cut it|he got|to do the
4 is to be|as it is|if we do|in all the|if we own it
```

All letters learned (Strike keys at a brisk, steady pace.)

```
5 Judy had gone for that big ice show at Lake Tahoe.
6 Jack said that all of you will find the right job.

7 Cindy has just left for work at the big ski lodge.
8 Rudy can take a good job at the lake if he wishes.
```

```
| 1  | 2  | 3  | 4  | 5  | 6  | 7  | 8  | 9  | 10 |
```

RD ◆ 15

Speed Check

1. Key each line once DS. To DS when in SS mode, strike **Return/Enter** twice at line ends.
2. Key a 20-second (20") timed writing on each line. Set the count-down timer *(MicroType Pro/Multimedia)*, Variable option (see p. viii); or have someone time you with a watch with a second hand.
3. Key another 20" writing on each line. Try to increase your keying speed.

Goal
At least 15 *gwam*.

Your rate in gross words a minute (*gwam*) is shown on this scale.

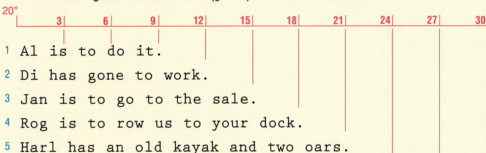

```
20"        3|     6|     9|    12|    15|    18|    21|    24|    27|    30
 1 Al is to do it.
 2 Di has gone to work.
 3 Jan is to go to the sale.
 4 Rog is to row us to your dock.
 5 Harl has an old kayak and two oars.
 6 She told us to set a goal and go for it.
 7 It is our job to see just how high we can go.
 8 Jake will go to the city to work on the big signs.
```

Enrichment

1. Key each line twice SS (slowly, then faster); DS between 2-line groups.
2. Rekey the drill for better control of reach-strokes.

```
1 Rob saw the bird on the lake by the big boat dock.
2 June had left for the club just as the news ended.
3 Bro led a task force whose goal was to lower cost.
4 Lyn knew the surf was too rough for kids to enjoy.
5 Ceil hikes each day on the side roads near school.
```

```
| 1  | 2  | 3  | 4  | 5  | 6  | 7  | 8  | 9  | 10 |
```

Lesson 19

New Keys: 9 and 4

Objectives:

1. To learn reach technique for 9 and 4.
2. To improve skill on straight copy, script, and rough draft.

19A◆ 5
Conditioning Practice
line spacing: SS
side margins: default

each line twice; then a 1' writing on line 3; find *gwam*

alphabet 1 Joby quickly fixed a glass vase and amazed the proud owners.

spacing 2 She told us to add the figures 11, 88, 18, 81, 118, and 881.

easy 3 Ciel may make a bid on the ivory forks they got in the city.

| 1 | 2 | 3 | 4 | 5 | 6 | 7 | 8 | 9 | 10 | 11 | 12 |

19B◆ 18
New Keys: 9 and 4

each line twice SS (slowly, then faster); DS between 2-line groups; if time permits, key lines 5-7 again

9 *Right ring* finger

4 *Left index* finger

Follow the *Standard Plan for Learning New Keys* outlined on p. 8.

Learn 9

use the letter "l"

1 l l 9l 9l ll 99 l9l l9l 99l 99l Reach up for 9, 99, and 999.

2 Key the figures 9, 99, and 999.   Did only 9 of 99 finish it?

Learn 4

3 f f 4f 4f ff 44 f4f f4f 44f 44f Reach up for 4, 44, and 444.

4 Add the figures 4, 44, and 444.   Please study pages 4 to 44.

Combine 9 and 4

5 Key 44, 49, 94, and 99.   Only 49 of the 94 joggers are here.

6 Reach with the fingers to key 49 and 499 as well as 4 and 9.

7 My goal is to sell 44 pizzas, 99 tacos, and 9 cases of cola.

19C◆ 5
New-Key Mastery

1. Key each of lines 1-3 twice SS (slowly, then faster); DS between 2-line groups.
2. If time permits, key each line again for speed.

Figure sentences

1 Keep the fingers low as you key 11, 18, 19, 48, 94, and 849.

use the figure "1"

2 On March 8, 1994, 14 people took the 4 tests for the 8 jobs.

3 He based his May 1 report on pages 449 to 488 of Chapter 19.

Lesson 10

New Keys: M and X

O b j e c t i v e s :

1. To learn reach technique for M and X.
2. To combine smoothly M and X with all other learned keys.

10A◆   7
Conditioning Practice

each line twice SS (slowly, then faster); DS between 2-line groups

reach review 1 bf ol rf yj ed nj ws ik tf hj cd uj gf by us if ow

b/y 2 by bye boy buy yes fib dye bit yet but try bet you

all letters learned 3 Robby can win the gold if he just keys a new high.

10B◆   20
New Keys: M and X

each line twice SS (slowly, then faster); DS between 2-line groups; if time permits, rekey lines 7-9

m *Right index* finger

x *Left ring* finger

Follow the *Standard Plan for Learning New Keys* outlined on p. 8.

Learn m

1 j j mj mj am am am me me ma ma jam jam ham ham yam

2 mj mj me me me may may yam yam dam dam men men jam

3 am to; if me; a man; a yam; a ham; he may; the hem

Learn x

4 s s xs xs ox ox ax ax six six fix fix fox fox axis

5 xs xs sx sx ox ox six six nix nix fix fix lax flax

6 a fox; an ox; fix it; by six; is lax; to fix an ax

Combine m and x

7 me ox am ax ma jam six ham mix fox men lax hem lox

8 to fix; am lax; mix it; may fix; six men; hex them

9 Mala can mix a ham salad for six; Max can fix tea.

18C◆ 16
New-Key Mastery

1. Key lines 1-12 once SS; DS between 2-line groups.
2. Key a 1' writing on line 13, then on line 14; find *gwam* on each writing.
3. If time permits, key a 1' writing on line 8 and then on line 12, trying to maintain your better rate in Step 2.

Technique goals

- reach *up* without moving the hand forward
- reach *down* without twisting the wrists or moving the elbows in and out

Row emphasis

figures	1 The quiz on the 18th will be on pages 11 to 18 and 81 to 88.
	2 Just 11 of the 118 boys got 81 of the 88 quiz answers right.
home/1st	3 hand axe | lava gas | can mask | jazz band | lack cash | a small flask
	4 Ms. Hamm can call a cab, and Max can flag a small black van.
home/3d	5 she quit | with just | that play | fair goal | will help | they did go
	6 Dru said you should try for the goal of top speed this week.

Response patterns

letter response	7 as in re on we no ax up gas oil red mop fee hum are you were
	8 You, in fact, saw him on a pump barge up at my mill at noon.
word response	9 if so is do id go us me am by an ox and the for men end form
	10 She is to go by the zoo to sign a work form for the six men.
combination response	11 if as so in is re do on go we us no me ax am up by pi an kin
	12 If she is at the inn, we may go by car to see a poppy field.
easy	13 Ty is to pay for the eight pens she laid by the audit forms.
	14 Keith is to row with us to the lake to fix six of the signs.

| 1 | 2 | 3 | 4 | 5 | 6 | 7 | 8 | 9 | 10 | 11 | 12 |

Skillbuilding

18D◆ 13
Speed Building

1. Key a 1' writing on each ¶; find *gwam* on each writing.
2. Add 2-4 *gwam* to better rate in Step 1 for a new goal.
3. Key three 1' guided writings on each ¶ at new goal rate. (See p. 45 for procedure.)

Quarter-Minute Checkpoints

gwam	1/4'	1/2'	3/4'	Time
16	4	8	12	16
20	5	10	15	20
24	6	12	18	24
28	7	14	21	28
32	8	16	24	32
36	9	18	27	36
40	10	20	30	40

e all letters used   2'

Do you think that someone is going to wait around just for   6
a chance to key your reports and paper? Do you believe that   13
when you work in an office there will be someone to key your   19
documents for you? Think again. The world does not work that 25
way.   26

Even a person in an important office position, such as the 32
head of a business, now operates the computer to send and get 38
data and to complete most day-to-day work. Be quick to realize 44
that you can get more done at work when you learn to key   51
with great skill. Be the best person at it and move up the   57
career ladder.   58

| 1 | 2 | 3 | 4 | 5 | 6 |

10C◆ 17
New-Key Mastery

1. Key each line once SS; DS between 2-line groups.
2. Key the lines again at a faster pace.

Technique goals

- reach *up* without moving hands away from you
- reach *down* without moving hands toward your body
- use quick-snap keystrokes

Goal: finger-action keystrokes; quiet hands and arms

3d/1st rows	1	by am end fix men box hem but six now cut gem ribs
	2	me ox buy den cub ran own form went oxen fine club
space bar	3	an of me do am if us or is by go ma so ah ox it ow
	4	by man buy fan jam can any tan may rob ham fun guy
key words	5	if us me do an sow the cut big jam rub oak lax boy
	6	curl work form born name flex just done many right
key phrases	7	or jam|if she|for me|is big|an end|or buy|is to be
	8	to fix|and cut|for work|and such|big firm|the call
all letters learned	9	Jacki is now at the gym; Lex is due there by four.
	10	Joni saw that she could fix my old bike for Gilda.

10D◆ 6
Technique: Spacing with Punctuation

each line once DS

> ### SPACING CUE:
> Do not space after an internal period in an abbreviation, such as Ed.D.

1 Mrs. Dixon may take her Ed.D. exam early in March.

2 Lex may send a box c.o.d. to Ms. Fox in St. Croix.

3 J. D. and Max will go by boat to St. Louis in May.

4 Owen keyed ect. for etc. and lost the match to me.

Enrichment

1. Key each line twice SS (slowly, then faster); DS between 2-line groups.
2. Key each line once more at a faster pace.

> ### PRACTICE CUE:
> Keep the insertion point moving steadily across each line (no pauses).

m/x	1	Max told them that he will next fix the main axle.
b/y	2	Byron said the boy went by bus to a bayou to hunt.
w/right shift	3	Will and Rona work in Tucson with Rowena and Drew.
u/c	4	Lucy cut a huge cake for just the four lucky boys.
w/left shift	5	Mr. and Mrs. J. L. Nance set sail for Long Island.
n/g	6	Bing may bring a young trio to sing songs at noon.
o/t	7	Lottie will tell the two little boys a good story.
i/r	8	Ria said she will first build a large fire of fir.
h/e	9	Chet was here when the eight hikers hit the trail.

UNIT 3

Learn Top-Row Technique: Figures
Lesson 18 New Keys: 8 and 1

Objectives:
1. To learn reach technique for 8 and 1.
2. To improve skill on straight copy, script, and rough draft.

18A◆ 5

Conditioning Practice

line spacing: SS
side margins: default

each line twice (slowly, then faster); a 1' writing on line 3; find *gwam*

alphabet 1 Max was quick to fly a big jet plane over the frozen desert.

spacing 2 Any of them can aim for a top goal and reach it if they try.

easy 3 Nan is to go to the city hall to sign the land forms for us.

| 1 | 2 | 3 | 4 | 5 | 6 | 7 | 8 | 9 | 10 | 11 | 12 |

18B◆ 16

New Keys: 8 and 1

each line twice (slowly, then faster); DS between 2-line groups; if time permits, key lines 5-7 again to build skill

8 *Right middle* finger

1 *Left little* finger

Follow the *Standard Plan for Learning New Keys* outlined on p. 8.

The Numeric Keyboarding section of *MicroType* contains lessons to match Unit 3.

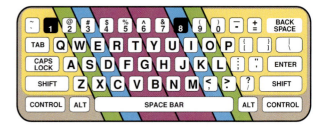

Learn 8

1 k k 8k 8k kk 88 k8k k8k 88k 88k Reach up for 8, 88, and 888.

2 Key the figures 8, 88, and 888. Please open Room 88 or 888.

Learn 1

3 a a 1a 1a aa 11 a1a a1a 11a 11a Reach up for 1, 11, and 111.

4 Add the figures 1, 11, and 111. Has just 1 of 111 finished?

Combine 8 and 1

5 Key 11, 18, 81, and 88. Just 11 of the 18 skiers have left.

6 Reach with the fingers to key 18 and 188 as well as 1 and 8.

7 The stock person counted 11 coats, 18 slacks, and 88 shirts.

Lesson 18

Lesson 11

New Keys: P and V

Objectives:

1. To learn reach technique for P and V.
2. To combine smoothly P and V with all other learned keys.

11A◆ 7
Conditioning Practice

each line twice SS (slowly, then faster); DS between 2-line groups

Fingers curved

Fingers upright

one-hand words 1 in we no ax my be on ad on re hi at ho cad him bet

phrases 2 is just|of work|to sign|of lace|to flex|got a form

all letters learned 3 Jo Buck won a gold medal for her sixth show entry.

11B◆ 20
New Keys: P and V

each line twice SS; DS between 2-line groups; if time permits, rekey lines 7-9

p *Right little* finger

v *Left index* finger

Follow the *Standard Plan for Learning New Keys* outlined on p. 8.

Learn p

1 ;   ; p; p; pa pa up up apt apt pen pen lap lap kept
2 p; p; pa pa pa pan pan nap nap paw paw gap gap rap
3 a pen; a cap; apt to pay; pick it up; plan to keep

Learn v

4 f f vf vf via via vie vie have have five five live
5 vf vf vie vie vie van van view view dive dive jive
6 go via; vie for; has vim; a view; to live; or have

Combine p and v

7 up cup vie pen van cap vim rap have keep live plan
8 to vie; give up; pave it; very apt; vie for a cup;
9 Vic has a plan to have the van pick us up at five.

Lesson 11

LEARN P AND V

32

Skillbuilding

17D◆ 10
Speed Building

line spacing: DS

1. Key one 1' unguided writing and two 1' guided writings on ¶ 1 as directed on p. 45.
2. Key ¶ 2 in the same way.
3. As time permits, key two 2' unguided writings on ¶s 1-2 together; find *gwam*.

Quarter-Minute Checkpoints			
gwam	**1/4'**	**1/2'**	**3/4' Time**
16	4	8	12 16
20	5	10	15 20
24	6	12	18 24
28	7	14	21 28
32	8	16	24 32
36	9	18	27 36
40	10	20	30 40

e all letters used

Are you one of the people who often look from the copy to the screen and down at your hands? If you are, you can be sure that you will not build a speed to prize. Make eyes on copy your next goal.

When you move the eyes from the copy to check the screen, you may lose your place and waste time trying to find it. Lost time can lower your speed quickly and in a major way, so do not look away.

17E◆ 12
Technique Mastery: Individual Letters

1. Key each line once; note the lines that caused you to slow down, hesitate, or stop altogether.
2. Key those lines two or three times to eliminate the hesitations and pauses.

Technique goals
- curved, upright fingers
- quick-snap keystrokes
- quiet hands and arms
- *finger* reaches with no finger "flyout"

P 1 Pepi popped up to a new pitcher but kept his cool.

Q 2 Qwen was quick to quote a quip to quiet the squad.

R 3 Rita wrote a big report for her course in history.

S 4 Sisi said she saw a flash before she heard a shot.

T 5 Toby took title to the truck after paying the fee.

U 6 Una is sure to turn a dull party into unusual fun.

V 7 Vic vexed five voters by vivid slogans on his van.

W 8 Wen will wash and wax two cars for the new lawyer.

X 9 Xena fixed a taxi axle for sixty dollars plus tax.

Y 10 Yanny says he may fly to your zany birthday party.

Z 11 Zaza dazzled us with zany jokes and bizarre humor.

11C ◆ 17
New-Key Mastery

1. Key the lines once SS; DS between 2-line groups.
2. Key the lines again at a faster pace.

Technique goals
- reach up without moving hands away from you
- reach down without moving hands toward your body
- use quick-snap keystrokes

Goal: finger-action keystrokes; quiet hands and arms

reach review	1	vf p; xs mj ed yj ws nj rf ik tf ol cd hj gf uj bf
	2	if lap jag own may she for but van cub sod six oak
3d/1st rows	3	by vie pen vim cup six but now man nor ton may pan
	4	by six but now may cut bent me fine gems five reps
key words	5	with kept turn corn duty curl just have worn plans
	6	name burn form when jury glad vote exit came eight
key phrases	7	if they⎮he kept⎮with us⎮of land⎮burn it⎮to name it
	8	to plan⎮so sure⎮is glad⎮an exit⎮so much⎮to view it
all letters learned	9	Kevin does a top job on your flax farm with Craig.
	10	Dixon flew blue jets eight times over a city park.

11D ◆ 6
Technique: Shift Keys and Return

Key a 1' writing on each 2-line sentence SS; DS between sentences.

Goal
To reach the end of each *line* in 30", someone using a watch with a second hand may call "Return" every 30". Or you may set the count-down timer (*MicroType*) for 30" and use an option (Display, Beep, or Flash) to help you meet the goal.

Eyes on copy as you shift and as you return

		30"	1'
1	Marv is to choose a high goal	12	6
2	and to do his best to make it.	12	12
3	Vi said she had to key from a book	14	7
4	as one test she took for a top job.	14	14
5	Lexi knows it is good to keep your goal	16	8
6	in mind as you key each line of a drill.	16	16
7	Viv can do well many of the tasks she tries;	18	9
8	she sets top goals and makes them one by one.	18	18

Enrichment

1. Key each line once at a steady, easy pace to master reach-strokes.
2. Key each line again at a faster pace.

Technique goals
- keep fingers upright
- keep hands/arms steady

m/p	1	mj p; me up am pi jam apt ham pen map ape mop palm
	2	Pam may pack plums and grapes for my trip to camp.
b/x	3	bf xs be ax by xi fix box but lax buy fox bit flax
	4	Bix used the box of mix to fix bread for six boys.
y/v	5	yj vf buy vow boy vie soy vim very have your every
	6	Vinny may have you buy very heavy silk and velvet.

Lesson 11

Lesson 17

Alphabetic Keying Technique

Objectives:
1. To learn proper response to different kinds of copy.
2. To develop control and speed on script and straight copy.

17A ◆ 5

Conditioning Practice

each line twice SS; then a 1'
writing on line 3; find *gwam*

alphabet	1	Wusov amazed them by jumping quickly from the box.
spacing	2	am to|is an|by it|of us|an oak|is to pay|it is due
easy	3	It is right for the man to aid them with the sign.

| 1 | 2 | 3 | 4 | 5 | 6 | 7 | 8 | 9 | 10 |

Skillbuilding

17B ◆ 18

Technique: Response Patterns

1. Key each set of 3 lines twice SS (slowly, then faster); DS between 6-line groups.
2. Key a 1' writing on line 10, on line 11, and on line 12; find *gwam* on each; compare rates.
3. If time permits, rekey the slowest line.

> **Combination response**
> Normal copy (as in lines 7-9) includes both word- and letter-response sequences, as described on p. 46. Use *top* speed for word response (easy words), *lower* speed for letter response (words that are harder to key).

letter response	1	be in as no we kin far you few pin age him get oil
	2	see him|was nil|vex you|red ink|wet mop|as you saw
	3	Milo saved a dazed polo pony as we sat on a knoll.
word response	4	ox if am to is may end big did own but and yam wit
	5	do it|to cut|he got|for me|jam it|an owl|go by air
	6	He is to go to the city and to do the work for me.
combination response	7	am at of my if on so as to be or we go up of no by
	8	am in|so as|if no|is my|is up|to be|is at|is up to
	9	Di was busy at the loom as you slept in the chair.
letter	10	Jon gazed at a phony scarab we gave him in a case.
combination	11	Pam was born in a small hill town at the big lake.
word	12	Keith is off to the lake to fish off the big dock.

| 1 | 2 | 3 | 4 | 5 | 6 | 7 | 8 | 9 | 10 |

17C ◆ 5

Handwritten Copy (Script)

Key the lines once DS (2 hard returns); rekey the lines if time permits.

1. Script is copy that is written with pen or pencil.
2. Copy that is written poorly is often hard to read.
3. Read script a few words ahead of the keying point.
4. Doing so will help you produce copy free of error.
5. Leave proper spacing after punctuation marks, too.
6. With practice, you will key script at a good rate.

Lesson 12

New Keys: Q and Comma (,)

O b j e c t i v e s :
1. To learn reach technique for Q and , (comma).
2. To combine smoothly Q and , (comma) with all other learned keys.

12A◆ 7
Conditioning Practice

each line twice SS (slowly, then faster); DS between 2-line groups; if time permits, rekey the lines

all letters learned	1	do fix all cut via own buy for the jam cop ask dig
p/v	2	a map; a van; apt to; vie for; her plan; have five
all letters learned	3	Beth will pack sixty pints of guava jam for David.

12B◆ 20
New Keys: Q and , (Comma)

each line twice SS; DS between 2-line groups; if time permits, rekey lines 7-9

q *Left little* finger

, (comma)
Right middle finger

SPACING CUE:
Space once after , used as punctuation.

Follow the *Standard Plan for Learning New Keys* outlined on p. 8.

Learn q

1 a qa qa aq aq quo quo qt. qt. quad quad quit quits
2 qa quo quo qt. qt. quay quay aqua aqua quite quite
3 a qt.; pro quo; a quad; to quit; the quay; a squad

Learn , (comma)

4 k k ,k ,k kit, kit; Rick, Ike, or I will go, also.
5 a ski, a ski; a kit, a kit; a kite, a kite; a bike
6 Ike, I see, is here; Pam, I am told, will be late.

Combine q and , (comma)

7 Enter the words quo, quote, quit, quite, and aqua.
8 I have quit the squad, Quen; Raquel has quit, too.
9 Marquis, Quent, and Quig were quite quick to quit.

Skillbuilding

16C◆   12
Speed Building
line spacing: DS

1. Key one 1' unguided and two 1' guided writings on ¶ 1 as directed on p. 45.
2. Key ¶ 2 in the same way.
3. As time permits, key two 2' unguided writings on ¶s 1-2 together; find *gwam*.

1' *gwam* goals
▽ 17 = acceptable
⊡ 21 = average
⊙ 25 = good
◇ 29 = excellent

e   all letters used   2'

　　　Keep in home position all of the fingers not   5
being used to strike a key. Do not let them move   10
out of position for the next letters in your copy.   15
　　　Prize the control you have over the fingers.   19
See how quickly speed goes up when you learn that   24
you can make them do just what you expect of them.   29

| 1 | 2 | 3 | 4 | 5 |

16D◆   15
Technique Mastery: Individual Letters

1. Key each line once; note the lines that caused you to slow down, hesitate, or stop altogether.
2. Key those lines two or three times to eliminate the hesitations and pauses.

Technique goals
- curved, upright fingers
- quick-snap keystrokes
- quiet hands and arms
- *finger* reaches with no finger "flyout"

The Keyboarding Skill Builder section of *MicroType Pro (Multimedia)* has drills similar to Lessons 16 and 17.

A 1 Alan had half a sandwich and a small salad at two.

B 2 Bobbi bought a big blue bow and bright red ribbon.

C 3 Cici can cut yucca and cactus for a class project.

D 4 Dodd did a wild dance to take a second gold medal.

E 5 Eve led her team to a new record in the last meet.

F 6 Fifi filed a full staff report at my field office.

G 7 Gig is going with a good group on the golf outing.

H 8 Hugh has had a huge lead in homers all this month.

I 9 Irena is in high spirits and is in medal position.

J 10 Jake adjusted a major jump just for the joy of it.

K 11 Kim baked cakes and cookies for a kooky ski party.

L 12 Lars blew his lead and finally fell to last place.

M 13 Mamie may make a major bid for many antique items.

N 14 Nat never knew how many friends he could count on.

O 15 Orpha lost a gold locket she wore to the town zoo.

12C◆ 17
New-Key Mastery

1. Key the lines once SS; DS between 2-line groups.
2. Key the lines again at a faster pace.

Technique goals
- reach *up* without moving hands away from you
- reach *down* without moving hands toward your body
- use quick-snap keystrokes

Goal: finger-action keystrokes; quiet hands and arms

reach review
1 qa .l ws ,k ed nj rf mj tf p; xs ol cd ik vf hj bf
2 yj gf hj quo vie pay cut now buy sot mix vow forms

3d/1st rows
3 six may sun coy cue mud jar win via pick turn bike
4 to go|to win|for me|a peck|a quay|by then|the vote

key words
5 pa rub sit man for own fix jam via cod oak the got
6 by quo sub lay apt mix irk pay when rope give just

key phrases
7 an ox|of all|is to go|if he is|it is due|to pay us
8 if we pay|is of age|up to you|so we own|she saw me

all letters learned
9 Jevon will fix my pool deck if the big rain quits.
10 Verna did fly quick jets to map the six big towns.

12D◆ 6
Technique: Spacing with Punctuation

each line once DS

SPACING CUE:
Space once after , and ; used as punctuation.

Space once.

1 Aqua means water, Quen; also, it is a unique blue.
2 Quince, enter qt. for quart; also, sq. for square.
3 Ship the desk c.o.d. to Dr. Quig at La Quinta Inn.
4 Q. J. took squid and squash; Monique, roast quail.

Enrichment

each set of lines twice SS (once slowly; then again at a faster pace); DS between 6-line groups

Technique goals
Lines 1-3:
fingers upright

Lines 4-6:
hands/arms steady

Lines 7-9:
two quick taps of each doubled letter

Adjacent keys

1 re io as lk rt jk df op ds uy ew vc mn gf hj sa ui
2 as ore ask opt buy pew say art owe try oil gas her
3 Sandy said we ought to buy gifts at her new store.

Long direct reaches

4 ce un gr mu br ny rv ym rb my ice any mug orb grow
5 nice curb must brow much fume sync many dumb curve
6 Brian must bring the ice to the curb for my uncle.

Double letters

7 all off odd too see err boo lee add call heed good
8 door meek seen huff less will soon food leek offer
9 Lee will seek help to get all food cooked by noon.

Lesson 12

UNIT 2

Lessons 16-17

Master Letter Keyboarding Technique
Lesson 16 Alphabetic Keying Technique

O b j e c t i v e s :
1. To learn proper response-pattern technique to gain speed.
2. To improve technique/speed on alphabetic copy.

16A◆   5
Conditioning Practice

each line twice SS; then a 1'
writing on line 3; find *gwam*

alphabet	1 Nat will vex the judge if she bucks my quiz group.
punctuation	2 Al, did you use these words: vie, zeal, and aqua?
easy	3 She owns the big dock, but they own the lake land.

| 1 | 2 | 3 | 4 | 5 | 6 | 7 | 8 | 9 | 10 |

Skillbuilding

16B◆   18
Technique: Response Patterns

1. Key each pair of lines twice SS; DS between 4-line groups.
2. Key a 1' writing on line 10 and then on line 12; find *gwam* (total words keyed) on each writing.
3. Key another 1' writing on the slower line to increase your speed on more difficult copy.

PRACTICE CUES:

Balanced-hand lines:
Think, say, and *key* the words by word response at a fast pace.
One-hand lines:
Think, say, and *key* the words by letter response at a steady but unhurried pace.

A **balanced-hand** word is one in which the letters of each 2-letter combination are keyed by opposite hands. In a **one-hand** word, all of the letters are keyed with the same hand.

Letter response
Many one-hand words (as in lines 3-4) are not easy to key. Such words may be keyed letter-by-letter and with continuity (steadily without pauses).

Word response
Short, balanced-hand words (as in lines 1-2) are so easy to key that they can be keyed as words, not letter-by-letter. *Think* and *key* them at your top speed.

balanced-hand words	1 ah do so go he us if is of or to it an am me by ox
	2 ha for did own the for and due pay but men may box
one-hand words	3 as up we in at on be oh ax no ex my ad was you are
	4 ad ink get ilk far him few pop set pin far imp car
balanced-hand phrases	5 of it|he is|to us|or do|am to|an ox|or by|is to do
	6 do the|and for|she did|all six|the map|for the pay
one-hand phrases	7 as on|be in|at no|as my|be up|as in|at him|saw you
	8 you are|oil tax|pop art|you get|red ink|we saw him
balanced-hand sentences	9 The man is to go to the city and do the auto work.
	10 The girl is to go by bus to the lake for the fish.
one-hand sentences	11 Jimmy saw you feed a deer on a hill up at my mill.
	12 Molly sat on a junk in oily waters at a bare reef.

| 1 | 2 | 3 | 4 | 5 | 6 | 7 | 8 | 9 | 10 |

Lesson 16

Review

Objectives:
1. To learn to key block paragraphs.
2. To improve keying technique and speed.

Fingers properly aligned

Fingers properly curved

RA◆ 7
Conditioning Practice

each line twice SS (slowly, then faster); DS between 2-line groups; if time permits, practice each line again

reach review 1 Virgil plans to find that mosque by six with Jack.

shift keys 2 Pam, Van, and Quin have to be in New Hope by five.

easy 3 Vi is to aid the girl with the sign work at eight.

| 1 | 2 | 3 | 4 | 5 | 6 | 7 | 8 | 9 | 10 |

RB◆ 10
Block Paragraphs

each paragraph (¶) once SS; DS between ¶s; then key the ¶s again at a faster pace

Your software will return automatically at the end of a line ("soft return"—also called "wordwrap"). So do not strike **Return/Enter** at the end of each line. Return twice at the end of ¶ 1 to leave a DS between ¶s. Your lines may end in a different place than the lines shown here.

Paragraph 1   1'

When you strike the return or enter key at the end   10
of a line to space down and start a new line, this   20
process is called a hard return.   27

Paragraph 2

If a machine returns at line ends for you, what is   10
known as a soft return or wordwrap is in use. You   20
must use a hard return, though, between paragraphs.   30

| 1 | 2 | 3 | 4 | 5 | 6 | 7 | 8 | 9 | 10 |

RC◆ 10
Speed Check

1. Key a 30' writing on each line. Your rate in gross words a minute (*gwam*) is shown word for word above the lines.
2. If time permits, key another 30' writing on each line. Try to increase your keying speed.

Goal: At least 18 *gwam*.

Reminder: The count-down timer (*MicroType*) may be used for the writings, or someone with a watch with a second hand may time you.

30' | 2 | 4 | 6 | 8 | 10 | 12 | 14 | 16 | 18 | 20 |

1 I am to fix the sign for them.

2 Jaye held the key to the blue auto.

3 Todd is to go to the city dock for fish.

4 Vi paid the girl to make a big bowl of salad.

5 Kal may keep the urn he just won at the quay show.

| 2| 4| 6| 8| 10| 12| 14| 16| 18| 20|

If you finish a line before time is up and start over, your *gwam* is the figure at the end of the line PLUS the figure above or below the point at which you stopped.

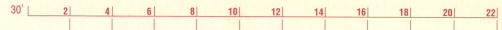

RC ◆ 8

Speed Check: Sentences

1. Key a 30' writing on each line. Your rate in *gwam* is shown word-for-word above the lines.
2. Key another 30' writing on each line. Try to increase your keying speed.

Goal
At least 22 *gwam*.

| | 30' | 2 | 4 | 6 | 8 | 10 | 12 | 14 | 16 | 18 | 20 | 22 |

1 He bid for the rich lake land.

2 Suzy may fish off the dock with us.

3 Pay the girls for all the work they did.

4 Quen is due by six and may then fix the sign.

5 Janie is to vie with six girls for the city title.

6 Duane is to go to the lake to fix the auto for the man.

| | 2 | 4 | 6 | 8 | 10 | 12 | 14 | 16 | 18 | 20 | 22 |

If you finish a line before time is up and start over, your *gwam* is the figure at the end of the line PLUS the figure above or below the point at which you stopped.

RD ◆ 15

Speed Check: Paragraphs

1. Key a 1' writing on each paragraph (¶); find *gwam* on each writing.
2. Using your better *gwam* as a base rate, select a goal rate and key two 1' guided writings on each ¶ as directed at bottom of page.

e all letters used   2'

| | 2 | | 4 | | 6 | | 8 | |

Tab → How you key is just as vital as the copy you   5

| 10 | | 12 | | 14 | | 16 | | 18 | |

work from or produce. What you put on paper is a   10

| 20 | | 22 | | 24 | | 26 | | 28 | |

direct result of the way in which you do the job.   15

| | 2 | | 4 | | 6 | | 8 | |

Tab → If you expect to grow quickly in speed, take   19

| 10 | | 12 | | 14 | | 16 | | 18 | |

charge of your mind. It will then tell your eyes   24

| 20 | | 22 | | 24 | | 26 | | 28 | |

and hands how to work through the maze of letters.   29

| 1 | 2 | 3 | 4 | 5 |

Quarter-Minute Checkpoints

gwam	1/4'	1/2'	3/4'	Time
16	4	8	12	16
20	5	10	15	20
24	6	12	18	24
28	7	14	21	28
32	8	16	24	32
36	9	18	27	36
40	10	20	30	40

Note: If you are not using *MicroType*, have someone using a watch with a second hand time you for a minute, calling *one-quarter* at 15", *one-half* at 30", *three-quarters* at 45", and *stop* at 60" (1 minute).

Guided Writing Procedure

Set a practice goal

1. Key a 1' writing on ¶ 1 above.
2. Using the *gwam* as a base, add 4 *gwam* to determine your goal rate.
3. Choose from Column 1 of the table at the left the speed nearest your goal rate. At the right of that speed, note the 1/4' points in the copy you must reach to maintain your goal rate.
4. Determine the checkpoint for each 1/4' from the word-count dots and figures above the lines in ¶ 1. (**Example:** Checkpoints for 24 *gwam* are 6, 12, 18, and 24.)

Practice procedure

1. Key two 1' writings on ¶ 1 at your goal rate guided by the Beep or Flash option in the count-down timer *(MicroType)*. See note at left.

Goal: To reach one of your checkpoints just as you hear a beep or see a flash.

2. Key two 1' writings on ¶ 2 in the same way.
3. If time permits, key a 2' writing on both ¶s together, without the guides.

Speed level of practice

When the purpose of practice is to reach out into new speed areas, use the *speed* level. Take the brakes off your fingers and experiment with new stroking patterns and new speeds. Do this by:

1. Reading 2 or 3 letters ahead of your keying to foresee stroking patterns.
2. Getting the fingers ready for the combinations of letters to be keyed.
3. Keeping your eyes on the copy in the book.

RD◆ 12

Technique: Space Bar and Shift Keys

each line twice SS; DS between 4-line groups

Goals

- to reduce the pause between words
- to reduce the time taken to shift/strike key/release when making capital letters

Down-and-in spacing

Out-and-down shifting

Space bar (Space *immediately* after each word.)

1 so an if us am by or ox he own jay pen yam own may
2 she is in|am to pay|if he may|by the man|in a firm

3 I am to keep the pens in a cup by a tan mail tray.
4 Fran may try to fix an old toy for the little boy.

Shift keys (Shift; strike key; release both quickly.)

5 J. V., Dr. or Mrs., Ph.D. or Ed.D., Fourth of July
6 Mrs. Maria Fuente; Dr. Mark V. Quin; Mr. T. C. Ott

7 B. J. Marx will go to St. Croix in March with Lex.
8 Mae has a Ph.D. from Miami; Dex will get his Ed.D.

RE◆ 11

Speed Building

each line twice SS (slowly, then faster); DS between 4-line groups

Technique goals

- quick-snap keystrokes
- quick joining of letters to form words
- quick joining of words to form phrases

Key words and phrases (*Think*, *say*, and *key* words and phrases.)

1 ox jam for oak rid pay got own the lap via sob cut
2 make than with them such they when both then their

3 to sit|an elf|by six|an oak|did go|for air|the jam
4 to vie|he owns|pay them|cut both|the quay|for they

Key sentences (Strike keys at a brisk, steady pace.)

all letters learned
5 I may have six quick jobs to get done for low pay.
6 Vicky packed the box with quail and jam for Signe.

all letters learned
7 Max can plan to bike for just five days with Quig.
8 Jim was quick to get the next top value for Debby.

Enrichment

1. Key each line once at a steady, easy pace.
2. Key each line again at a faster pace.

Technique goals

- keep fingers upright
- keep hands/arms steady

q/b
1 qa bf by quo but qt. quit both quad lube quid blow
2 Bob quickly won my squad over quip by brainy quip.

x/,
3 xs ,k sxs k,k ox ox, six six, flax flax, axle axle
4 I keyed ox, six, lox, mix, fox, fix, fax, and nix.

p/m
5 p; mj p.m. map amp pep mum mop imp camp ramp clump
6 Palma and her mom made peppy caps for my pep team.

v/y
7 vf yj ivy vary envy very wavy navy have many savvy
8 Levy may have to vary the way we serve and volley.

Review

O b j e c t i v e s :
1. **To demonstrate level of technique mastery.**
2. **To demonstrate level of keying speed attained.**

RA◆ 7
Conditioning Practice

each line twice SS; then a 1'
writing on line 3; find *gwam*

alphabet 1 Quig just fixed prize vases he won at my key club.

spacing 2 Marcia works for HMS, Inc.; Juanita, for XYZ Corp.

easy 3 Su did vow to rid the town of the giant male duck.

| 1 | 2 | 3 | 4 | 5 | 6 | 7 | 8 | 9 | 10 |

RB◆ 20
Technique Check

each line twice SS; DS between
6-line groups

Fingers curved

Fingers upright

Finger-action key-stroking

Down-and-in spacing

Reach review (Keep on home keys the fingers not used for reaching.)

1 old led kit six jay oft zap cod big laws five ribs

2 pro quo|is just|my firm|was then|may grow|must try

3 Olga sews aqua and red silk to make six big kites.

Space bar emphasis (*Think*, *say*, and *key* the words.)

4 en am an by ham fan buy jam pay may form span corn

5 I am|a man|an elm|by any|buy ham|can plan|try them

6 I am to form a plan to buy a firm in the old town.

Shift key emphasis (Reach *up* and reach *down* without moving the hands.)

7 Jan and I are to see Ms. Han. May Lana come, too?

8 Bob Epps lives in Rome; Vic Copa is in Rome, also.

9 Oates and Co. has a branch office in Boise, Idaho.

Easy sentences (*Think*, *say*, and *key* the words at a steady pace.)

10 Eight of the girls may go to the social with them.

11 Corla is to work with us to fix the big dock sign.

12 Keith is to pay the six men for the work they did.

| 1 | 2 | 3 | 4 | 5 | 6 | 7 | 8 | 9 | 10 |

New Keys: Z and Colon (:)

Objectives:
1. To learn reach technique for Z and : (colon).
2. To combine smoothly Z and : (colon) with all other learned keys.

13A◆ 7
Conditioning Practice

each line twice SS; then a 1'
writing on line 3; find *gwam*

> **Note:** Whenever directions in this book call for a timed writing, you may use the count-down timer in your *MicroType* software. (This note will not appear again.)

all letters learned   1   Jim won the globe for six quick sky dives in Napa.

spacing   2   to own|is busy|if they|to town|by them|to the city

easy   3   She is to go to the city with us to sign the form.

    | 1 | 2 | 3 | 4 | 5 | 6 | 7 | 8 | 9 | 10 |

13B◆ 18
New Keys: Z and :
(Colon)

each line twice SS (slowly,
then faster); DS between
2-line groups; if time permits,
rekey lines 7-10

z **Left little** *finger*

: (colon) **Left Shift** *then*
right little *finger*

LANGUAGE SKILLS CUE:
Space twice after : used as punctuation. Capitalize the first word of a complete sentence following a colon.

Follow the *Standard Plan for Learning New Keys* outlined on p. 8.

Learn z
1 a a za za zap zap zap zoo zoo zip zip zag zag zany
2 za za zap zap zed zed oz. oz. zoo zoo zip zip maze
3 zap it, zip it, an adz, to zap, the zoo, eight oz.

Learn : (colon)
4 ; ; :; :; Date: Time: Name: Room: From: File:
5 :; :; To: File: Reply to: Dear Al: Shift for :
6 Two spaces follow a colon, thus: Try these steps:

Combine z and : (colon)
7 Zelda has an old micro with : where ; ought to be.
8 Zoe, use as headings: To: Zone: Date: Subject:
9 Liza, please key these words: zap, maze, and zoo.
10 Zane read: Shift to enter : and then space twice.

15C◆ 10
Technique: Space Bar, Shift Keys, and CAPS LOCK

each pair of lines twice SS; DS between 4-line groups

Fingers upright

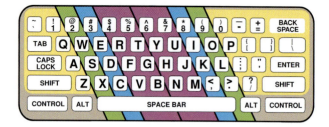

space bar
1 an me so en if em by he ox go am do is no or in to
2 She may go to the city if he can fix the old auto.

shift key
3 The best dancers are: Ana and Jose; Mag and Boyd.
4 Did Ms. Paxon send us the letter from Dr. LaRonde?

CAPS LOCK
5 Masami saw the game on ESPN; Krista saw it on NBC.
6 The AMS meeting is on Tuesday; the DPE, on Friday.

15D◆ 14
Speed Building

1. Key the lines once SS; DS between 2-line groups.
2. Key a 1' writing on each of lines 5-8; find *gwam* on each writing (1' *gwam* = total 5-stroke words keyed).
3. If time permits, key another 1' writing on line 7 and then on line 8 for speed.

Key words and phrases (*Think*, *say*, and *key* words and phrases.)

1 ad my we in be on at up as no are him was you gets
2 girl quay turn rush duty down maps rich laid spend

3 an ad|to fix|an oak|to get|the zoo|via jet|in turn
4 if they|to risk|by them|the duty|and paid|she kept

Key easy sentences (Key the words at a brisk, steady pace.)

5 He is to aid the girls with the work if they wish.
6 Jan may go to the city for the bid forms for them.

7 He may go to the lake by dusk to do the dock work.
8 I did all the work for the firm for the usual pay.

| 1 | 2 | 3 | 4 | 5 | 6 | 7 | 8 | 9 | 10 |

15E◆ 7
Speed Check

1. Key each ¶ once SS; DS between ¶s. Use wordwrap.
2. Key a 1' writing on each ¶; find *gwam* on each writing. (1' *gwam* = figure above the last word keyed—the dots represent odd numbers)

Copy used to measure skill is triple-controlled for difficulty. An **e** shows that these ¶s are easy.

 all letters used

        •   2   •   4   •   6   •   8   •

    Be quick to excel in form and speed. If you
10   •   12   •   14   •   16   •   18
do, you can move back a word or two and watch the
20   •   22   •   24   •   26   •   28   •
errors fall away. Keep this in mind as you work.

      •   2   •   4   •   6   •   8
    You might be amazed how your speed will grow
10   •   12   •   14   •   16   •   18
if you first push for speed and then level off to
20   •   22   •   24   •   26   •   28
take control at just the right speed. Try it now.

Lesson 15

13C◆ 15
New-Key Mastery

1. Key the lines once SS; DS between 2-line groups.
2. Key the lines again at a faster pace.

Technique goals
- curved, upright fingers
- quiet hands and arms
- steady key stroking pace

Fingers properly aligned

q/z
1 zoo qt. zap quo zeal quay zone quit maze quad hazy
2 Zeno amazed us all on the quiz but quit the squad.

p/x
3 apt six rip fix pens flex open flax drop next harp
4 Lex is apt to fix apple pie for the next six days.

v/m
5 vim mum van dim have move vamp more dive time five
6 Riva drove them to the mall in my vivid lemon van.

easy
7 Glen is to aid me with the work at the dog kennel.
8 Dodi is to go with the men to audit the six firms.

alphabet
9 Nigel saw a quick red fox jump over the lazy cubs.
10 Jacky can now give six big tips from the old quiz.

13D◆ 10
Block Paragraphs

1. Key each paragraph (¶) once SS; DS between them; then key them again faster.
2. Key a 1' writing on each ¶; find your *gwam*.

Paragraph 1   1'

The space bar is a vital tool, for every fifth or   10
sixth stroke is a space when you key. If you use   20
it with good form, it will aid you to build speed.   30

Paragraph 2

Just keep the thumb low over the space bar. Move   10
the thumb down and in quickly toward your palm to   20
get the prized stroke you need to build top skill.   30

| 1 | 2 | 3 | 4 | 5 | 6 | 7 | 8 | 9 | 10 |

Enrichment

1. Key each line once at a steady, easy pace.
2. Key each line again at a faster pace.

Technique goals
- keep fingers upright
- keep hands/arms steady

x/:
1 xs :; | fix mix | Max: Use TO: and FROM: as headings.
2 Read and key: oxen, exit, axle, sixty, and sixth.

q/,
3 qa ,k | aqa k,k | quo quo, | qt. qt., | quite quite, | squat
4 Quen, key these: quit, aqua, equal, quiet, quick.

p/z
5 p; za | ;p; zaza | zap zap | zip zip | size size | lazy lazy
6 Zip put hot pepper on his pizza at the zany plaza.

m/v
7 mj vf | jmj fvf | vim vim | vow vow | menu menu | move movie
8 Mavis vowed to move with a lot more vim and vigor.

Lesson 15

Tab Key

15A ◆   7

Conditioning Practice

each line twice SS; then a
1' writing on line 3; find *gwam*

> CAPS LOCK affects only the
> letter keys; shifted punctua-
> tion marks—such as : and
> ?—require the use of one of
> the shift keys.

Fingers properly curved

alphabet 1 Zosha was quick to dive into my big pool for Jinx.

CAPS LOCK 2 Type these ZIP Codes: OR, MD, RI, NV, AL, and PA.

easy 3 Ian kept a pen and work forms handy for all of us.

| 1 | 2 | 3 | 4 | 5 | 6 | 7 | 8 | 9 | 10 |

15B ◆   12

Paragraph Indention

The **Tab key** is used to indent
copy. Software uses preset tabs
(called **default** tabs).

Usually, the first default tab is set
0.5' to the right of the left margin
and is used to indent ¶s
(see copy below right).

1. Locate the Tab key on your keyboard (usually at upper left of alphabetic keyboard).
2. Reach up to the Tab key with the left little finger; strike the key firmly and release it quickly. The insertion point will move 0.5' to the right.
3. Key each ¶ once SS, using soft returns; DS between ¶s. As you key, strike the Tab key firmly to indent the first line of each ¶.
4. If you complete all ¶s, rekey them as time permits.

Tab key *Left little* **finger**

Tab →The tab key is used to indent blocks of copy such as these.

Tab → It should also be used for tables to arrange data quickly and neatly into columns.

Tab →Learn now to use the tab key by touch; doing so will add to your keying skill.

Tab→ Strike the tab key firmly and release it very quickly. Begin the line without a pause.

Tab → If you hold the tab key down, the cursor will move from tab to tab across the line.

Lesson 14
New Keys: CAPS LOCK and Question Mark (?)

Objectives:
1. To learn reach technique for CAPS LOCK and ? (question mark).
2. To combine smoothly CAPS LOCK and ? (question mark) with other learned keys.

14A◆ 7
Conditioning Practice

each line twice SS; then a 1' writing on line 3; find *gwam*

alphabet 1 Lovak won the squad prize cup for sixty big jumps.

z/: 2 To: Ms. Mazie Pelzer; From: Dr. Eliza J. Piazzo.

easy 3 He is to go with me to the dock to do work for us.

| 1 | 2 | 3 | 4 | 5 | 6 | 7 | 8 | 9 | 10 |

14B◆ 16
New Keys: CAPS LOCK and ? (Question Mark)

each line twice SS (slowly, then faster); DS between 2-line groups; if time permits, rekey lines 7-9

CAPS LOCK
Left little finger

? (question mark)
Left Shift then *right little* finger

Depress CAPS LOCK to key a series of capital letters. To release CAPS LOCK to key lowercase letters, strike CAPS LOCK key again.

Learn CAPS LOCK

1 Hal read PENTAGON and ADVISE AND CONSENT by Drury.

2 Oki joined FBLA when her sister joined PBL at OSU.

3 Zoe now belongs to AMS and DPE as well as to NBEA.

Learn ? (question mark)

Space twice.

4 ; ; ?; ?; Who? What? When? Where? Why? Is it?

5 Who is it? Is it she? Did he go? Was she there?

6 Is it up to me? When is it? Did he key the line?

Combine CAPS LOCK and ?

7 Did he join a CPA firm? I will stay on with NASA.

8 Is her dad still CEO at BSFA? Or was he made COB?

9 Did you read HOMEWARD? If so, try WHIRLWIND next.

14C◆ 18
New-Key Mastery

1. Key the lines once SS; DS between 2-line groups.
2. Key the lines again at a faster pace.
3. Key a 1' writing on line 11 and then on line 12; find *gwam* on each writing.

Technique goals

■ reach *up* without moving hands away from you

■ reach *down* without moving hands toward your body

> **TECHNIQUE CUE:**
> Use CAPS LOCK to make ALL CAPS.

To find 1' *gwam* : Add 10 for each line you completed to the scale figure beneath the point at which you stopped in a partial line.

Goal: finger-action keystrokes; quiet hands and arms

CAPS LOCK/?	1	Did she join OEA? Did she also join PSI and DECA?
	2	Do you know the ARMA rules? Are they used by TVA?
z/v	3	Zahn, key these words: vim, zip, via, zoom, vote.
	4	Veloz gave a zany party for Van and Roz in La Paz.
q/p	5	Paul put a quick quiz on top of the quaint podium.
	6	Jacqi may pick a pink pique suit of a unique silk.
key words	7	they quiz pick code next just more bone wove flags
	8	name jack flax plug quit zinc wore busy vine third
key phrases	9	to fix it|is to pay|to aid us|or to cut|apt to own
	10	is on the|if we did|to be fit|to my pay|due at six
alphabet	11	Lock may join the squad if we have six big prizes.
easy	12	I am apt to go to the lake dock to sign the forms.

| 1 | 2 | 3 | 4 | 5 | 6 | 7 | 8 | 9 | 10 |

14D◆ 9
Block Paragraphs

1. Key each paragraph once, using soft returns. The lines you key will be longer than the lines shown if default side margins are used. DS between ¶s.
2. If time permits, key a 1' writing on one or two of the paragraphs.

Goal

Continuity (keep the insertion point moving steadily across the screen).

> Insert at least four hard returns between 1' writings to avoid confusion when you find *gwam*.

1'

Paragraph 1
When you key lines of drills, strike the return or   10
enter key at the end of each line. That is, use a   20
hard return to space down for a new line.   29

Paragraph 2
When you key copy in this form, though, you do not   10
need to return at the end of each line because the   20
software ends every full line with a soft return.   30

Paragraph 3
Even though your software returns or wraps at line   10
endings, you do have to strike the enter or return   20
key at the end of a paragraph to have a blank line.   31

Paragraph 4
Learn now when you do not need to return at ends   10
of lines and when you must do so. Doing this now   20
will assure that your copy will be in proper form.   30

| 1 | 2 | 3 | 4 | 5 | 6 | 7 | 8 | 9 | 10 |

Lesson 14

Activity 1
Center

1. Read the copy at right.
2. Find the Justification features/buttons for your wp software.
3. Key the 6 lines at the right DS so that they are centered horizontally.

 Use this feature for the main heading of a report (p. A7).

Justification refers to the horizontal position of a line of text. Use the **Center** feature to center one or more lines of text between the left and right margins.

Conservation Laws

Newton's Law of Gravity

Relativity and the Nuclear Age

The Solar System

Elements, Compounds, and States of Matter

The Atmosphere and Meteorology

Activity 2
Delete

1. Read the copy at right.
2. Learn how to delete text using your wp software.
3. Key the ¶ at the right DS; underline text as shown as you key.
4. Using the most efficient method, delete all underlined text.
5. Edit as needed to correct spacing.

The **delete** or **backspace** key may be used to correct simple keying errors. For deleting a word or phrase, however, a combination of keys and the mouse is faster. For example, in some wp packages the **Ctrl + Backspace** deletes a word (left of the insertion point) and the **Ctrl + Delete** deletes a group of words (right of the insertion point).

John Homer, Naomi Kerrit, <u>Paul Desmond</u>, and Kay Ford were selected by the <u>five</u> geology faculty members to make a <u>short multimedia</u> presentation at the <u>upcoming</u> Delaware Valley Geological Society <u>meeting</u> on January 5 at the Harris Hotel in Clarks Summit. <u>They will fly into Philadelphia from Columbus.</u>

Activity 3
Undelete and Undo

1. Read the copy at right.
2. Learn how to use the Undo and Undelete features of your wp software.
3. Key the ¶ at the right DS using bold as shown.
4. Read the ¶ you keyed; then undo and undelete as directed in it.

Use the **Undo** feature/button to reverse the last change you made in text. (Some wp packages undo only the most recent editing change.) Undo restores text to its original location, even if you have moved the insertion point to another position. **Undelete**, a feature available on some wp packages, restores deleted text at the insertion point. Undelete usually allows you to restore any or all of the last three deletions.

After keying **this** paragraph, delete **the** bolded words and restore them at their original place. Now: If your **wp** software has an Undelete feature, delete the words Now and Next (delete : too). Next: Restore the word Now (with :) at the beginning of the paragraph and the word Next before the last sentence. Correct spacing between sentences and after colons.

A word processor is an excellent tool that can help you demonstrate your best writing skills. When you use a word processor to write papers for school, your final draft is likely to reflect your best effort.

The ease with which you can add, delete, and cut and paste copy with word processors encourages you to write a series of drafts until you know you have done your best.

The use of the word processor's spell checker, thesaurus, and grammar checker will "help" you to identify spelling, grammar, and punctuation errors; find and use the correct word; and identify style flaws.

Activity 6
Center Page

1. Read the copy at right.
2. Learn to center copy vertically using your wp software.
3. Open a new file (File menu, New). Set side margins at 2" (see p. xv).
4. Use the Center Page feature.
5. Key the ¶s at the right DS.
6. Keep this text on the screen and proceed to Activity 7.

[wp] Use this feature for business letters (p. A6) instead of spacing down 2" to key the dateline.

Use the **Center Page** feature to center lines of text between the top and bottom margins of a page, if the page is not full. This feature leaves an equal (or nearly equal) amount of white space above and below the text.

Activity 5
Copy and Move

1. Read the copy at right.
2. Learn how to copy and move text using your wp software.
3. Key the four ¶s as shown at right.
4. Copy the 1st ¶ and place it as the 5th ¶.
5. Move the 2d ¶ so it is the 4th ¶; move what is now the 3d ¶ so it becomes the 2d ¶.
6. Edit so that ¶s are SS with DS between, and no ¶ indention.

The Move feature is commonly called "cut and paste," and the Copy feature is often called "copy and paste."

The Block feature is used in the move and copy commands in the same way it is used to bold, italicize, center, or delete text.

Most word processing software has button bars that can be used to cut, copy, and paste text quickly.

The text will be moved or copied to the insertion point that is selected when the "paste" command is executed.

Activity 4
Block

1. Read the copy at right.
2. Learn how to block text using your wp software. Also find the Bold and Italics features/buttons on your software near the Underline feature/button.
3. Key the 6 lines.
4. Follow directions shown at the end of each line, using the Block feature.

Use the **Block** feature to select a block of text on which various operations may be performed. A block of text can be bolded, italicized, underlined, deleted, centered, copied, moved, printed, saved, etc. A block is selected by clicking or sweeping the mouse to highlight the text. Once blocked, the

After you have blocked text, you can use the Cut and Paste or Copy features. The **Cut** feature/button removes blocked text from one location and the **Paste** feature/button places it in another location. The **Copy** feature/button duplicates (copies) the blocked text. The **Paste** feature/button places it at another location, leaving the original unchanged.

1. The office of Best & Jones will be relocated soon. (Bold **Best & Jones**)
2. Mary and Jane confused there and their in the report. (Italicize *and*; underline there, their)
3. Twelve computers and five printers arrived yesterday. (Bold **computers, printers**)
4. The students just started reading A Man for All Seasons. (Underline book title)
5. Death of a Salesman was written by Arthur Miller. (Italicize play title)
6. Tom and Mary saw the parade and then went to the circus. (Delete last six words, center the line)

Activity 7
Speller

1. Read the copy at right.
2. Learn to use your wp software's Speller.
3. Use the Speller to check the text keyed in Activity 6. Correct all errors found by editing or choosing a replacement offered by the Speller.
4. Proofread after Speller is used. Correct any errors you find. (Keep this text on screen.)

 Use Speller on every document that you key, but follow up with proofreading for other kinds of errors.

Use the **Speller** to check words, documents, or parts of documents for misspellings. A Speller checks a document by comparing each word to words in its dictionary. If the Speller finds a word in your document that is not identical to one in its dictionary, the word is displayed in a dialog box. Usually the Speller lists words it "believes" are likely corrections (replacements) for the displayed word. When a word is displayed, you must choose to do one of the following:

1. Retain the spelling of the word as it is displayed in the dialog box and add it to the Speller's dictionary.
2. Replace a misspelled word that is displayed with a correctly spelled word offered by the Speller.
3. Replace a misspelled word that is displayed by editing it if the Speller does not list the correctly spelled replacement.

Spellers often use similar procedures for checking repeated words and/or irregular capitalizations.

Activity 8
View

1. Read the copy at right.
2. Learn how to preview a document using your wp software.
3. Preview the document from Activity 7 to see how it will look on a printed page.

It is a good practice to see how your document will look on paper before it is printed. Most wp software has a View (or Preview) feature that lets you do so. Thus you will not waste time and paper printing a document that is unattractive. The view (or preview) mode will display a miniature of each page. In some software, a document can be edited in this mode. If needed, the "zoom" feature can be used to enlarge parts of a document for a closer look.

Activity 9
Flush Right

1. Read the copy at right.
2. Find the Flush Right feature/button on your wp software (near or combined with the Center feature/button).
3. Key your name so that it is right-justified.
4. Key the lines in Items 1-3 at the right.

 Flush Right may be used to place a page number at the right margin in a report (p. A8).

Use the **Flush Right** feature/button when you want a line of text (or part of a line) to end even with the right margin. Flush Right can be activated before or after text is keyed. If turned on before text is keyed, the text will "back up" from the right margin as you type.

1. Use Flush Right, then key each line.

This line is keyed with Flush Right activated.
This line uses Flush Right so that it ends at the right.

2. Key each line at left margin as shown, block the four lines, and use Flush Right to align them at the right margin.

Massey Hall
Room 315
Phone: (715) 167-8045
Fax: (715) 167-8145

3. Key each line (begin at left margin); use Flush Right to place only the ZIP + 4 at the right margin.

375 Baker Street, Jamestown, New York 14701-7598
960 Pembroke Street, New Rochelle, New York 10801-3127

Activity 10
Date

1. Read the copy at right.
2. Learn the Date Text and Date Code features for your wp software.
3. Key the lines at the right using the Date Text and Date Code features as indicated.

Today's date can be inserted into a document by using the **Date Text** feature. The **Date Code** feature also inserts the current date into the document. However, the Date Code feature replaces the previous date with the current date each time the document is opened or printed. The date and time on your computer must be current for the date to be correct.

<Date Text>
Mr. Jason Winchell
428 North 500 West
Salt Lake City, UT 84103-8321

<Date Code>
Ms. Rochelle Wilson
351 Parkwood Cir.
Anderson, SC 29621-8256

Activity 11
Hyphenation

1. Read the copy at right.
2. Learn to use the Hyphenation feature.
3. Key the text at the right with hyphenation off.
4. Key the text again with hyphenation on.

wp Check spelling using the Speller feature. Edit or replace words that contain errors.

The **Automatic Hyphenation** feature divides (hyphenates) words that normally would wrap to the next line. This gives the right margin of the document a more attractive appearance.

A very useful feature in most of today's best word processing software packages is the feature that automatically hyphenates long words at the right margin. This feature will automatically divide such words rather than wrap them to the next line. By dividing these words automatically, the hyphenation feature makes the right margin less "ragged."

Activity 12
Scrolling

1. Read the copy at right.
2. Learn to move the insertion point using **Home, End, PgDn, PgUp,** and **Home** (Ctrl)+ **arrow key** or **arrow key** combinations.
3. Key Sentence 1; edit as instructed in Sentences 2, 3, and 4 using the arrow keys.

The **Home, End, PgUp,** and **PgDn** keys can be used to move the insertion point quickly from one location to another location in a document.

The **Home** or **Ctrl** key in combination with the arrow keys can also be used to move the insertion point rapidly.

1. Key the following.

   Ellen will be in New York on Monday.

2. Make the following changes, using the arrow keys.

   Ellen will be in New York on Monday.
   [handwritten: Castino, Albany, June 25]

3. Make these additional changes, utilizing the arrow keys.

   Ellen Castino will be in Albany, New York, on Monday, June 25.
   [handwritten: Ms., the manager, Tuesday, 26]

4. Make these changes.

   Ms. Ellen Castino, the manager, will be in Albany, New York, on Tuesday, June 26 *[handwritten: new; from 11 a.m. to 3 p.m.]*

TO: **Tab** **Tab** Faculty and Staff   **2" (line 13)**

DS (2 hard returns)

FROM: **Tab** Lenore M. Fielding, Principal **DS**

DATE: **Tab** (Today's date) **DS**

SUBJECT: **Tab** STANDARD MEMO FORMAT **DS**

At a recent meeting, department heads recommended that memos be processed on plain paper instead of preprinted forms. This recommendation is a cost-cutting measure that requires only a little more effort on the part of the keyboard operator. **DS**

The customary standard margins are used: 2" top margin; default (near 1") side margins; at least a 1" bottom margin. **DS**

 Standard double spacing separates memo parts, including para- graphs, which are individually single-spaced. If someone other than the writer keys the memo, that person's initials should be keyed at the left margin a double space below the message. If an attachment or enclosure is included, <u>Attachment</u> or <u>Enclosure</u> should be keyed at the left margin a double space below the message or the keyboard operator's initials (if any). **DS**   **1"**

Headings begin at left margin. After TO: tab twice to key the name; after FROM: tab once to key the name; after DATE: tab once to key the date; after SUBJECT: space twice (or tab once) to enter the subject (may be keyed in ALL CAPS or C/lc--Cap and lowercase). **DS**

Please use this format for several days; then let me know if you experienced any difficulties. **DS**

tbh

Standard Memo

---

wp The default top margin is likely 1". Insert six hard returns to space down another inch.

Suggestions:

- Use the Date feature (Activity 10) for the memo date.
- Use the Delete (Activity 2) and Undelete/Undo (Activity 3) features as needed when keying the memo.
- Use the Speller (Activity 7). Edit or replace words identified as errors.

- Proofread (on screen). Use Scrolling fea- tures (Activity 12) to move the insertion point to each error.
- At the top of the page, turn on hyphenation (Activity 11).
- View the document (Activity 8) to see how it will look on paper.

Business Letter in Block Format

Kendal Computers

738 St. Louis St.   ▲   Baton Rouge, LA 77802-3615   ▲   Office: 504-555-1278   ▲   Fax: 504-555-1998

Dateline — (Today's date)   2" or use Center Page

QS (4 hard returns)

Letter address —
Mr. Julio M. Basanez, Manager
La Paloma Restaurant
224 Saint Louis St.
Baton Rouge, LA 77802-3615

DS

Salutation — Dear Julio

DS

Body — Your piquant black bean soup drew me back to the La Paloma yesterday. We were taken promptly to our table, but we waited over ten
minutes before menus were presented.

DS

Several times I provided clues to the server that I was hosting the
luncheon. Without noting these clues or asking who should receive
the check, the server gave it to the man across from me. Had the
check been placed upside down in the middle of the table, my client
wouldn't have been "put on the spot."

DS

Several times a week someone from my company entertains clients at
La Paloma Restaurant. Will you talk with your staff about greeting
diners promptly and about handling checks properly. But please,
Julio, don't disturb the chef!

DS

Complimentary close — Cordially   QS (4 hard returns)

Mrs. Luanne Chang

Writer — Mrs. Luanne Chang, President

DS

Reference initials — mt   As the keyboard operator, you key your
initials here.

See Suggestions, p. A5.

COMPUTER APPLICATIONS

Title

QS (2 DS)

Learning to key is of little value unless one applies it in preparing a useful document--a letter, a report, and so on. Three basic kinds of software (applications) are available to assist those with keying skill in applying that skill electronically.

Report body

DS

Side heading
Word Processing Software

DS

Word processing software is specifically designed to assist in the document preparation needs of individuals or businesses. Word processing software permits the user to "create, edit, format, store, and print documents." (Fulton and Hanks, 1996, 152) The software can be used to process a wide variety of documents such as memos, letters, reports, and tables.

Textual citation

This software has editing and formatting features that reduce time and effort. It permits easy error detection and correction; merging of text with variables in another document or even another application (for example, database software); and graphic design of pages. These features increase efficiency while enhancing the appearance of documents.

1" LM

1" RM

DS

Side heading
Database Software

DS

A database is any collection of related items stored in computer memory. The data in a database may be about club members, employee payroll, company sales, and so on. Database software allows the user to enter data, sort it, retrieve and change it, or select certain data (such as an address) for use in word processing documents. (Tilton, et al, 1996, 112-113)

Textual citation

Unbound Report with Textual Citations

At least 1"

(continued on next page)

Unbound Report with Textual Citations, Page 2

Page number

2 ← Page number

Side heading

Spreadsheet Software ← Side heading
DS

A spreadsheet is an electronic worksheet made up of columns and rows of data. Spreadsheet software allows the user to "create, calculate, edit, retrieve, modify, and print graphs, charts, reports, and spreadsheets" necessary for current business operations and in planning for the future. (Fulton and Hanks, 1996, 156) ← Textual citation

1" LM → A review of newspaper advertisements shows the skills that employers expect for most jobs: competent use of word processing and spreadsheet software and familiarity with database applica- ← 1" RM
tions.
QS (2 DS)

REFERENCES
QS

Fulton, Patsy, J., and Joanna D. Hanks. Procedures for the Office ← List of references
Professional. 3d ed. Cincinnati: South-Western Publishing
Co., 1996.
DS
Tilton, Rita S., et al. The Electronic Office: Procedures &
Administration. 11th ed. Cincinnati: South-Western Publish-
ing Co., 1996.

Repetitive stress injury (RSI) is a result of repeated movement of a particular part of the body. A familiar example is "tennis elbow." Of more concern to keyboard users is the form of RSI called **carpal tunnel syndrome (CTS)**.

CTS is an inflammatory disease that develops gradually and affects the wrists, hands, and forearms. Blood vessels, tendons, and nerves pass into the hand through the carpal tunnel (see illustration below). If any of these structures enlarge or if the walls of the tunnel narrow, the median nerve is pinched, and CTS symptoms may result.

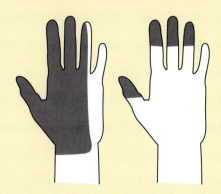

Areas affected by carpal tunnel syndrome

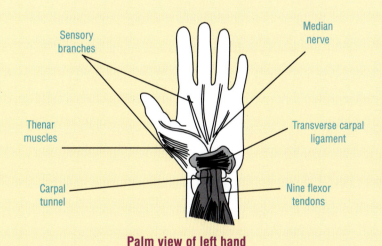

Palm view of left hand

Labels: Sensory branches, Median nerve, Thenar muscles, Transverse carpal ligament, Carpal tunnel, Nine flexor tendons

Causes of RSI/CTS

RSI/CTS often develops in workers whose physical routine is unvaried. Common occupational factors include: (1) using awkward posture, (2) using poor techniques, (3) performing tasks with wrists bent (see below), (4) using improper equipment, (5) working at a rapid pace, (6) not taking rest breaks, and (7) not doing exercises that promote graceful motion and good techniques.

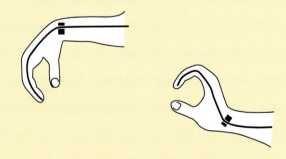

Improper wrist positions for keystroking

Symptoms of RSI/CTS

CTS symptoms include numbness in the hand; tingling or burning in the hand, wrist, or elbow; severe pain in the forearm, elbow, or shoulder; and difficulty in gripping objects. Symptoms usually appear during sleeping hours, probably because many people sleep with their wrists flexed.

If not properly treated, the pressure on the median nerve, which controls the thumb, forefinger, middle finger, and half the ring finger (see top right), causes severe pain. The pain can radiate into the forearm, elbow, or shoulder and can require surgery or result in permanent damage or paralysis.

Other factors associated with CTS include a person's genetic makeup; the aging process; hormonal influences; obesity; chronic diseases such as rheumatoid arthritis and gout; misaligned fractures; and hobbies such as gardening, knitting, and woodworking that require the same motion over and over. CTS affects over three times more women than men, with 60 percent of the affected persons between the ages of 30 and 60.

Reducing the Risk of RSI/CTS

Carpal tunnel syndrome is frequently a health concern for workers who use a computer keyboard or mouse. The risk of developing CTS is less for computer keyboard operators who use proper furniture and equipment, keyboarding techniques, posture, and/or muscle-stretching exercises than for those who do not.

Keyboard users can reduce the risk of developing RSI/CTS by taking these precautions.

1. Arrange the workstation correctly:
   a. Position the keyboard directly in front of the chair.
   b. Keep the front edge of the keyboard even with the edge of the desk or table so that the wrist movement will not be restricted while you are keying.
   c. Position the keyboard at elbow height.
   d. Position the monitor about 18 to 24 inches from your eyes with the top edge of the display screen at eye level.
   e. Position the mouse next to and at the same height as the computer keyboard and as close to the body as possible.

2. Use a proper chair and sit correctly:
   a. Use a straight-backed chair, or adjust your chair so that it will not yield when you lean back.
   b. Use a seat that allows you to keep your feet flat on the floor while you are keying. Use a footrest if your feet cannot rest flat on the floor.
   c. Sit erect and as far back in the seat as possible.

3. Use correct arm and wrist positions and movement:
   a. Keep your forearms parallel to the floor and level with the keyboard so that your wrists will be in a flat, neutral position rather than flexed upward or downward.
   b. Keep arms near the side of your body in a relaxed position.

4. Use proper keyboarding techniques:
   a. Keep your fingers curved and upright over the home keys.
   b. Keep wrists and forearms from touching or resting on any surface while keying.
   c. Strike each key lightly using the fingertip. Do not use too much pressure or hold the keys down.

5. When using a keyboard or mouse, take short breaks. A rest of one to two minutes every hour is appropriate. Natural breaks in keyboarding action of several seconds' duration also help.

6. Exercise the neck, shoulder, arm, wrist, and fingers before beginning to key each day and often during the workday (see No. 5). Suggested exercises for keyboard users are described below. You can do all the exercises while sitting at your workstation.

Exercises for Keyboard Users

1. *Strengthen finger muscles.* (See Drill 1 on p. A11.) Open your hands, extend your fingers wide, and hold with muscles tense for two or three seconds; close the fingers into a tight fist with thumb on top, holding for two or three seconds; relax the fingers as you straighten them. Repeat 10 times. Additional finger drills are shown on p. A11.

2. *Strengthen the muscles in the carpal tunnel area.* While sitting with your arms comfortably at your side and hands in a fist, rotate your hands inward from the wrist. Repeat this motion 10 to 15 times; then rotate outward from the wrist 10 to 15 times. Extend your fingers and repeat the movements for the same number of times.

3. *Loosen forearms.* With both wrists held in a neutral position (not bent) and the upper arm hanging vertically from the shoulder, rotate both forearms in 15 clockwise circles about the elbow. Repeat, making counterclockwise circles.

4. *Stretch the arms.* Interlace the fingers of both hands, with the palms facing forward; stretch your arms in front of you and hold for ten seconds. Repeat at least once. Next, with your fingers still interlaced, stretch your arms over your head and hold for ten seconds. Repeat at least once.

5. *Loosen elbows.* Place your hands on your shoulders with elbows facing forward; slowly move your arms in increasingly larger circles in front of you 10 to 15 times.

6. *Relieve shoulder tension.* Interlace the fingers of both hands behind your head and slowly move the elbows back, pressing the shoulder blades together; hold for ten seconds. Repeat at least once.

Finger Gymnastics

Brief daily practice of finger gymnastics will strengthen your finger muscles and increase the ease with which you key. Begin each keying period with this conditioning exercise. Choose two or more drills for this practice.

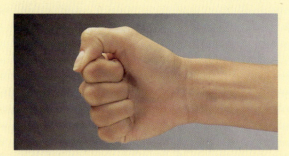

DRILL 1. Hands open, fingers wide, muscles tense. Close the fingers into a tight fist, with thumb on top. Relax the fingers as you straighten them; repeat 10 times.

DRILL 2. Clench the fingers as shown. Hold the fingers in this position for a brief time; then extend the fingers, relaxing the muscles of fingers and hand. Repeat the movements slowly several times. Exercise both hands at the same time.

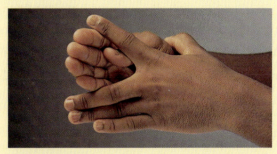

DRILL 3. Place the fingers and the thumb of one hand between two fingers of the other hand, and spread the fingers as much as possible. Spread all fingers of both hands.

DRILL 4. Interlace the fingers of the two hands and wring the hands, rubbing the heel of the palms vigorously.

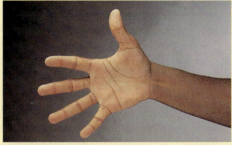

DRILL 5. Spread the fingers as much as possible, holding the position for a moment or two; then relax the fingers and lightly fold them into the palm of the hand. Repeat the movements slowly several times. Exercise both hands at the same time.

DRILL 6. Rub the hands vigorously. Let the thumb rub the palm of the hand. Rub the fingers, the back of the hand, and the wrist.

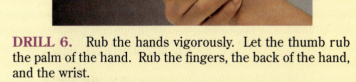

DRILL 7. Hold both hands in front of you, fingers together. Hold the last three fingers still and move the first finger as far to the side as possible. Return the first finger; then move the first and second fingers together; finally move the little finger as far to the side as possible.

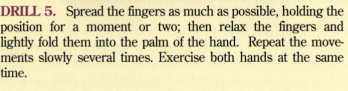

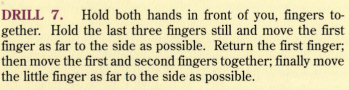

Capitalization Guides

Capitalize

1. The first word of every sentence and the first word of every complete direct quotation. Do not capitalize (a) fragments of a quotation or (b) a quotation resumed within a sentence.
   She said, "Hard work is necessary for success."
   He stressed the importance of "a sense of values."
   "When all else fails," he said, "follow directions."

2. The first word after a colon if that word begins a complete sentence.
   Remember this: Work with good techniques.
   We carry these sizes: small, medium, and large.

3. First, last, and all other words in titles of books, articles, periodicals, headings, and plays, except words of four or fewer letters used as articles, conjunctions, or prepositions.
   Century 21 Keyboarding   "How to Buy a House"
   Saturday Review   "The Sound of Music"

4. An official title when it precedes a name or when used else-where if it is a title of distinction.
   President Lincoln   She is the Prime Minister.
   The doctor is in.   He is the class treasurer.

5. Personal titles and names of people and places.
   Miss Franks   Dr. Jose F. Ortez   San Diego

6. All proper nouns and their derivatives.
   Canada   Canadian Festival   France   French food

7. Days of the week, months of the year, holidays, periods of history, and historic events.
   Sunday   Labor Day   New Year's Day
   June   Middle Ages   Civil War

8. Geographic regions, localities, and names.
   the North   Upstate New York   Mississippi River

9. Street, avenue, company, etc., when used with a proper noun.
   Fifth Avenue   Avenue of the Stars   Armour & Co.

10. Names of organizations, clubs, and buildings.
    Girl Scouts   4-H Club   Carew Tower

11. A noun preceding a figure except for common nouns such as line, page, and step, which may be keyed with or without a capital.
    Style 143   Catalog 6   page 247   step 3

12. Seasons of the year only when they are personified.
    icy fingers of Winter   the soft kiss of Spring

Number Expression Guides

Use words for

1. Numbers from one to ten except when used with numbers above ten, which are keyed as figures. Note: Common business practice is to use figures for all numbers except those that begin a sentence.
   Was the order for four or eight books?
   Order 8 shorthand books and 15 English books.

2. A number beginning a sentence.
   Fifteen persons are here; 12 are at home sick.

3. The shorter of two numbers used together.
   ten 50-gallon drums   350 five-gallon drums

4. Isolated fractions or indefinite amounts in a sentence.
   Nearly two-thirds of the students are here.
   About twenty-five people came to the meeting.

5. Names of small-numbered streets and avenues (ten and under).
   1020 Sixth Street   Tenth Avenue

Use figures for

1. Dates and time, except in very formal writing.
   May 9, 2002   10:15 a.m.
   ninth of   four o'clock

2. A series of fractions.
   Key 1/2, 1/4, 5/6, and 7 3/4.

3. Numbers following nouns.
   Rule 12   page 179   Room 1208   Chapter 15

4. Measures, weights, and dimensions.
   6 ft. 9 in. tall   5 lbs. 4 oz.   8 1/2" x 11"

5. Definite numbers used with the percent sign (%); but spell out approximate amounts. Spell out percent with approximate amounts and in all formal writing.
   The rate is 15 1/2%.
   About fifty percent of the work is done.

6. House numbers except house number One.
   1915 - 42d Street   One Jefferson Avenue

7. Amounts of money. Even amounts may be keyed without the decimal. Amounts of a million and over may be keyed as shown.
   $10.75   25 cents   seven hundred dollars ($700)
   $300 $12 million

Punctuation Guides

Use an apostrophe

1. As a symbol for *feet* or *minutes* on forms or charts. (The quotation mark may be used as a symbol for *seconds* or *inches*.)

   12' x 16'   3' 54"   8' 6" x 10' 8"

2. To indicate the omission of letters or figures (as in contractions).

   can't   I'll   we're   Spirit of '76

3. To form the plural of most figures, letters, and words used as words rather than for their meaning: Add the *apostrophe* and *s*. In market quotations, form the plural of figures by the addition of *s* only.

   6's   A's   five's   ABC's   Century Fund 4s

4. To show possession: Add the *apostrophe* and *s* to (a) a singular noun and (b) a plural noun which does not end in *s*.

   a man's watch   women's shoes   boy's bicycle

   Add the *apostrophe* and *s* to a proper name of one syllable that ends in s.

   Bess's Cafeteria   James's hat   Jones's bill

   Add the *apostrophe only* after (a) plural nouns ending in *s* and (b) a proper name of more than one syllable that ends in *s* or *z*.

   boys' camp   Adams' home   Melendez' report

   Add the *apostrophe* after the last noun in a series to indicate joint or common possession by two or more persons; however, add the possessive to each of the nouns to show separate possession by two or more persons.

   Lewis and Clark's expedition
   the manager's and the treasurer's reports

Use brackets

1. To enclose examples, explanations, etc., within parentheses.

   Mail is sorted by scanners (optical character readers [OCR's]) at the post office.

2. To show that you altered quoted copy in some minor way.

   "To attach oneself to [a] place is to surrender to it, and *suffer with it*." [Italics added]

Use a colon

1. To introduce an enumeration or a listing.

   These poets are my favorites: Shelley, Keats, and Frost.

2. To introduce a question or a long direct quotation.

   This is the question: Did you study for the test?

3. Between hours and minutes expressed in figures.

   10:15 a.m.   12:00   4:30 p.m.

Use a comma (or commas)

1. After (a) introductory phrases or clauses and (b) words in a series.

   If you plan to be here for the week, try to visit Chicago, St. Louis, and Dallas.

2. To set off short direct quotations.

   She said, "If you try, you can reach your goal."

3. Before and after (a) words that come together and refer to the same person, thing, or idea and (b) words of direct address.

   Clarissa, our class president, will give the report.
   I was glad to see you, Terrence, at the meeting.

4. To set off nonrestrictive clauses (not necessary to the meaning of the sentence), but not restrictive clauses (necessary to the meaning).

   Your report, which deals with the issue, is great.
   The girl who just left is my sister.

5. To separate the day from the year and the city from the state.

   July 4, 2000   New Haven, Connecticut

6. To separate two or more parallel adjectives (adjectives that could be separated by the word "and" instead of the comma).

   a group of young, old, and middle-aged persons

   Do not use commas to separate adjectives so closely related that they appear to form a single element with the noun they modify.

   a dozen large red roses   a small square box

7. To separate (a) unrelated groups of figures that come together and (b) whole numbers into groups of three digits each (however, *policy, year, page, room, telephone,* and most *serial numbers* are shown without commas).

   During 1998, 1,750 cars were insured under Policy 806423.
   page 1042   Room 1184   (213) 125-2626

Use a dash

1. For emphasis.

   The icy road—slippery as a fish—was a hazard.

2. To indicate a change of thought.

   We may tour the Orient—but I'm getting ahead of my story.

3. To introduce the name of an author when it follows a direct quotation.

   "Hitting the wrong key is like hitting me."—Armour

4. For certain special purposes.

   "Well—er—ah," he stammered.
   "Jay, don't get too close to the —." It was too late.

Punctuation Guides (cont.)

Use an ellipsis

1. To show the omission of one or more words within or at the end of a quoted sentence.
   "I'd seen something that my teacher . . . could not see."
   "It's as if they're free to speak with their true voice . . ."
2. To show faltering speech.
   Well . . . I mean . . . Who would have thought . . . ?

Use an exclamation point

1. After emphatic interjections.
   Wow!   Hey there!   What a day!
2. After sentences that are clearly exclamatory.
   "I won't go!" she said with determination.
   How good it was to see you in New Orleans last week!

Use a hyphen

1. To join compound numbers from twenty-one to ninety-nine that are keyed as words.
   forty-six   fifty-eight   over seventy-six
2. To join compound adjectives before a noun that they modify as a unit.
   well-laid plans   six-year period   two-thirds majority
3. After each word or figure in a series of words or figures that modify the same noun (suspended hyphenation).
   first-, second-, and third-class reservations
4. To spell out a word or name.
   s-e-p-a-r-a-t-e   S-u-s-a-n   G-a-e-l-i-c
5. To form certain compound nouns.
   WLW-TV   teacher-counselor   AFL-CIO

Use parentheses

1. To enclose parenthetical or explanatory matter and added information.
   The amendments (Exhibit A) are enclosed.
2. To enclose identifying letters or figures in lists.
   Check these factors: (1) period of time, (2) rate of pay, and (3) nature of duties.
3. To enclose an abbreviation following the first occurrence of a long name.
   File Form 1096 with the Internal Revenue Service (IRS) by March 1.

Use a question mark

At the end of a sentence that is a direct question; however, use a period after a request in the form of a question.
What day do you plan to leave for Honolulu?
Will you mail this letter for me, please.

Use quotation marks

1. To enclose direct quotations.
   He said, "I'll be there at eight o'clock."
2. To enclose titles of articles and other parts of complete publications, short poems, song titles, television programs, and unpublished works like theses and dissertations.
   "Sesame Street"   "Chicago" by Sandburg
   "Lara's Theme"   "Murder She Wrote"
3. To enclose special words or phrases, or made-up words.
   "power up" procedure   "Murphy's Law"

Use a semicolon

1. To separate two or more independent clauses in a compound sentence when the conjunction is omitted.
   Being critical is easy; being constructive is not so easy.
2. To separate independent clauses when they are joined by a conjunctive adverb (however, consequently, etc.).
   I can go; however, I must get excused.
3. To separate a series of phrases or clauses (especially if they contain commas) that are introduced by a colon.
   These officers were elected: Lu Ming, President; Lisa Stein, vice president; Juan Ramos, secretary.
4. Before expressions that start an explanation of the main clause.
   She organized her work, for example, putting work to be done in folders of different colors to indicate degrees of urgency.

Use an underline

1. With titles of complete works such as books, magazines, and newspapers. (Such titles may also be keyed in ALL CAPS or italic without the underline.)
   Smoky Night   The New York Times   TV Guide
2. To call attention to special words or phrases (or you may use quotation marks). (Note: Use a continuous underline unless each word is to be considered separately.)
   Stop keying when time is up.
   Spell these words: steel, occur, separate.

Basic Grammar Guides

Use a singular verb

1. With a singular subject.

   The weather is clear but cold.

2. With an indefinite pronoun (*each, any, either, neither, one,* etc.) used as a subject.

   Each of you is to bring a pen and paper.
   Neither of us is likely to be picked.

3. With singular subjects linked by *or* or *nor*. If, however, one subject is singular and the other is plural, the verb should agree with the *closer* subject.

   Either Jan or Fred is to make the presentation.
   Neither the principal nor the teachers are here.

4. With a collective noun (*committee, team, class, jury,* etc.) if the collective noun acts as a unit.

   The jury has returned to the courtroom.
   The committee has filed its report.

5. With the pronouns *all* and *some* (as well as fractions and percentages) when used as subjects if their modifiers are singular. Use a plural verb if their modifiers are plural.

   All of the books have been classified.
   Some of the gas is being pumped into the tank.

6. When *number* is used as the subject and is preceded by *the*; however, use a plural verb if *number* is preceded by *a*.

   The number of voters has increased this year.
   A number of workers are on vacation.

Use a plural verb

1. With a plural subject.

   The blossoms are losing their petals.

2. With a compound subject joined by *and*.

   My mother and my father are the same age.

Negative forms of verbs

1. Use the plural verb *do not* (or the contraction *don't*) when the pronoun *I, we, you,* or *they*, or a plural noun, is used as the subject.

   You don't have a leg to stand on in this case.
   The scissors do not cut properly.
   I don't believe that answer is correct.

2. Use the singular verb *does not* (or the contraction *doesn't*) when the pronoun *he, she,* or *it*, or a singular noun, is used as the subject.

   She doesn't want to attend the meeting.
   It does not seem possible that winter's here.

Pronoun agreement with antecedents

1. Pronouns (*I, we, you, he, she, it, their,* etc.) agree with their antecedents *in person*—person speaking, first person; person spoken to, second person; person spoken about, third person.

   We said we would go when we complete our work.
   When you enter, present your invitation.
   All who saw the show found that they were moved.

2. Pronouns agree with their antecedents *in gender* (feminine, masculine, and neuter).

   Each of the women has her favorite hobby.
   Adam will wear his favorite sweater.
   The tree lost its leaves early this fall.

3. Pronouns agree with their antecedents *in number* (singular or plural).

   A verb must agree with its subject.
   Pronouns must agree with their antecedents.
   Brian is to give his recital at 2 p.m.
   Joan and Carla have lost their homework.

4. When a pronoun's antecedent is a collective noun, the pronoun may be either singular or plural depending on whether the noun acts individually or as a unit.

   The committee met to cast their ballots.
   The class planned its graduation program.

Commonly confused pronoun sound-alikes

it's (contraction): it is; it has
its (possessive adjective): possessive form of *it*

It's good to see you; it's been a long time.
The puppy wagged its tail in welcome.

their (pronoun): possessive form of *they*
there (adverb/pronoun): at or in that place
they're (contraction): they are

The hikers all wore their parkas.
Will he be there during our presentation?
They're likely to be late because of the snow.

who's (contraction): who is; who has
whose (pronoun): possessive form of *who*

Who's been to the movie? Who's going now?
I chose the one whose skills are best.

2-LETTER STATE ABBREVIATIONS

Alabama	AL	Guam	GU	Massachusetts	MA	New York	NY	Tennessee	TN
Alaska	AK	Hawaii	HI	Michigan	MI	North Carolina	NC	Texas	TX
Arizona	AZ	Idaho	ID	Minnesota	MN	North Dakota	ND	Utah	UT
Arkansas	AR	Illinois	IL	Mississippi	MS	Ohio	OH	Vermont	VT
California	CA	Indiana	IN	Missouri	MO	Oklahoma	OK	Virgin Islands	VI
Colorado	CO	Iowa	IA	Montana	MT	Oregon	OR	Virginia	VA
Connecticut	CT	Kansas	KS	Nebraska	NE	Pennsylvania	PA	Washington	WA
Delaware	DE	Kentucky	KY	Nevada	NV	Puerto Rico	PR	West Virginia	WV
District of Columbia	DC	Louisiana	LA	New Hampshire	NH	Rhode Island	RI	Wisconsin	WI
Florida	FL	Maine	ME	New Jersey	NJ	South Carolina	SC	Wyoming	WY
Georgia	GA	Maryland	MD	New Mexico	NM	South Dakota	SD		

FOLDING PROCEDURES

Small Envelopes (Nos. 6 3/4, 6 1/4)
1. With page face up, fold bottom up to 0.5" from top.
2. Fold right third to left.
3. Fold left third to 0.5" from last crease.
4. Insert last creased edge first.

Large Envelopes (Nos. 10, 9, 7 3/4)
1. With page face up, fold slightly less than one-third of sheet up toward top.
2. Fold down top of sheet to within 0.5" of bottom fold.
3. Insert last creased edge first.

Window Envelopes (Letter)
1. With page face down, top toward you, fold upper third down.
2. Fold lower third up so address is showing.
3. Insert sheet into envelope with last crease at bottom.
4. Check that address shows through window.

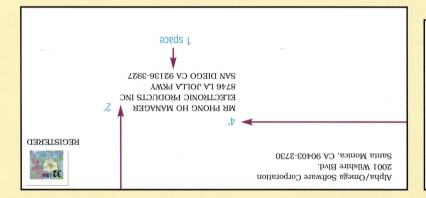

ENVELOPE GUIDES

The Envelope function on word processing software places addresses as described and shown below. (Exception: Mailing notations cannot be added by the Envelope function.)

If the function is used while a letter is open, the software "reads" the letter address and places it on the envelope. You may need to specify envelope size, type of paper feed for your printer, your choice of font, etc.

You can choose to print a POSTNET bar code above or below the envelope address. A machine-readable form of ZIP Code + 4, bar codes speed mail sorting at the post office.

Return Address

Use block style, SS, and Caps/lowercase. Begin on line 2 from top of envelope, 3 spaces from left edge.

Envelope Address

Set a tab 2.5" from left edge of small envelope and 4" from left edge of large envelope. Space down about 2" from top edge of envelope; begin address at tab position.

USPS (Postal Service) Style

Use block style, SS. Use ALL CAPS; omit punctuation. An address must contain three lines. Omit nonessential information to avoid more than six lines. Place ONLY the city name, 2-letter state abbreviation, and ZIP Code + 4 on last address line. One space precedes the ZIP Code.

Mailing Notations

Place notations that affect postage, such as SPECIAL DELIVERY and REGISTERED, a DS below the stamp in ALL CAPS.

Place addressee notations, such as HOLD

International Addresses

Omit postal (ZIP) codes from the last line of addresses outside the U.S. Show only the name of the country on the last line. Examples:

MS INGE D FISCHER
HARTMANNSTRASSE 7
4209 BONN 5
FEDERAL REPUBLIC OF GERMANY

MR HIRAM SANDERS
2121 CLEARWATER ST
OTTAWA ONK1A 0B1
CANADA

Standard Abbreviations

Use USPS standard abbreviations for states (see list below) and street suffix names, such as AVE and BLVD. Never abbreviate the name of a city or country.

FOR ARRIVAL or PERSONAL, a DS below the return address in ALL CAPS.